Teaching the Selected Works of Walter Dean Myers

The Young Adult Novels in the Classroom Series

When former Heinemann–Boynton/Cook editor Peter Stillman first conceived the Young Adult Literature (YAL) series in 1990 and asked me to be the series editor, I was excited to be part of such an innovative endeavor. At that time there were few professional books available for teachers who wanted to bring young adult literature into their classrooms, and Heinemann was the first publisher making a concerted effort to fill this need. Seventeen years and many books later, under the direction of Heinemann Executive Editor Lisa Luedeke, the series continues to inform and assist teachers at the middle school, high school, and college levels as they read with and teach to their students the best works that the field of young adult literature has to offer.

The Heinemann YAL Series takes another step forward with the book you hold in your hands. This subseries on teaching the works of specific young adult authors is designed to help you incorporate young adult literature into your curriculum, providing ideas and lessons that you may use and offering examples of classroom-tested student work, lesson plans, and discussion as an impetus to designing your own lessons and developing your own ideas in accordance with your students' needs.

Over the years, many teachers in my graduate young adult literature classes have asked me how to convince administrators and parents that young adult literature is worthy of a place in the curriculum alongside the classics and other commonly taught literary works. In response I have shown them how to write rationales for specific books, how to design lesson plans and units that satisfy state and national standards, how to deal with censorship, and how to become connoisseurs of young adult literature themselves. I hope that the books in this subseries, by focusing on specific authors of young adult literature and highlighting the successful work of teachers with this genre, will inspire confidence in you to bring these extraordinary works into your curriculum, not just as a bridge to the classics, but as literary works in their own right.

—Virginia R. Monseau

Teaching the Selected Works of Robert Cormier

Teaching the Selected Works of Mildred D. Taylor

Teaching the Selected Works of Katherine Paterson

Teaching the Selected Works of Walter Dean Myers

Teaching the Selected Works of Gary Paulsen (forthcoming)

Teaching the Selected Works of Chris Crutcher (forthcoming)

Teaching the
Selected Works of
Walter Dean Myers

Connie S. Zitlow

HEINEMANN
PORTSMOUTH, NH

Heinemann
A division of Reed Elsevier Inc.
361 Hanover Street
Portsmouth, NH 03801–3912
www.heinemann.com

Offices and agents throughout the world

Library of Congress Cataloging-in-Publication Data
Zitlow, Connie S., 1942–
    Teaching the selected works of Walter Dean Myers / Connie S. Zitlow.
        p. cm. — (The young adult novels in the classroom series)
    Includes bibliographical references.
    ISBN-13: 978-0-325-00886-8
    ISBN-10: 0-325-00886-8
    1. Myers, Walter Dean, 1937– —Study and teaching. 2. Myers, Walter
Dean, 1937– —Criticism and interpretation. 3. Young adult literature,
American—Study and teaching. 4. Children's literature, American—Study
and teaching. I. Title.

PS3563.Y48Z95 2007
813'.54—dc22   2007016382

Editor: Virginia R. Monseau
Production management: Lisa S. Garboski, bookworks publishing services
Production coordination: Vicki Kasabian
Cover design: Night & Day Design
Typesetter: Tom Allen, Pear Graphic Design
Manufacturing: Steve Bernier

Printed in the United States of America on acid-free paper
11 10 09 08 07   VP   1 2 3 4 5

CONTENTS

ACKNOWLEDGMENTS

Although I didn't know it at the time, this book began when I first attended an Assembly on Literature for Adolescents (ALAN) workshop, became friends with Virginia Monseau, and participated in the excitement of talking about young adult literature with countless authors, teachers, librarians, students, and my colleagues in teacher education. Books, particularly the works classified as young adult literature, have continued to be the focus of much of my scholarly work and teaching. As a professor of Education and the director of the Adolescence to Young Adult Licensure Program at Ohio Wesleyan University in Delaware, Ohio, I have had the pleasure of observing in many middle and high school classrooms while working with student teachers and the gifted teachers who served as cooperating teachers.

It is a pleasure to highlight the work of some of these outstanding teachers and acknowledge their generosity in welcoming me into their classrooms. I am grateful to teachers Maggie Massaro and Judy Hollander and teacher/librarian Karen Hildebrand at Dempsey Middle School, who so willingly shared their ideas about the Walter Dean Myers Unit they teach each year, and to teachers Zana Adams and Christopher Moore at Olentangy Liberty High School, who use *Fallen Angels* as the central work in their units about war. I also wish to acknowledge the many students who answered my questions and shared their work with me. I hope I have conveyed some of the depth of how reading the wonderful literary works of Walter Dean Myers has enriched their lives. As these teachers and students know, his books certainly have an important place as part of the middle and high school curriculum.

INTRODUCTION

Walter Dean Myers, a premier author of books for children and young adults, has published more than 100 literary works since 1968 when he won a writing contest for the text of his first picture book, *Where Does the Day Go?*, published in 1969. His productivity is astounding, both in numbers of literary works and in the variety of genres in which he publishes: fiction, poetry, short stories, a play, picture books, a memoir, and works of nonfiction that include history, biography, and some of his own genealogy. His works have received numerous awards, including Newbery Honors, *Boston Globe–Horn Book* Honors, and numerous Coretta Scott King Awards. His books frequently appear on lists of the best books of the year by organizations such as the American Library Association and are chosen as New York Public Library Books for the Teen Age. Walter Dean Myers received the first Michael L. Printz Award for *Monster*, a work that was also a National Book Award Finalist. For his body of work, he was honored with the Assembly on Literature for Adolescents (ALAN) Award, the Margaret A. Edwards Award, and the Virginia Hamilton Literary Award. He is a gifted, compassionate, introspective, humble person who speaks and writes with eloquence and a sincerity that has endeared him to readers of all ages.

Significant as a literary artist and an accomplished storyteller, Walter Dean Myers is also important as a black male writer who consistently publishes books for teens. In his humble way, he refers to his writing as talking to himself and letting children listen. His ear for dialogue, his use of rich imagery, and his careful choice of language bring to life his memorable characters as readers see, hear, and smell the richness of the vivid settings of his stories. He attributes his love of reading and writing to his early experiences: "My formal education began in the Harlem apartment of my foster parents, Herbert and Florence Dean," he stated in his essay "And Then I Read . . ." (2001a, 58). After her day's work was done, his foster mother would read to him from *True Romance* magazines. He learned that written words had meanings that he could translate into oral vocabulary and therefore understand. Even when he was very young, he and his mother had real conversations as they talked about where they would go on their walks and what they would do together.

Walter Dean Myers learned to read before entering school. But school was a misery to him because of his speech impediment, something he has since learned was genetic. In school his classmates laughed and teased him; his response was to lash out and fight. Because reading in front of the class was the worst part of his life, he learned to write poetry using words that he knew he could pronounce. When Mrs. Conway, his fifth-grade teacher, caught him reading comic books, she took them away and gave him a stack of "good" books to read. That was the same year he not only spent time playing ball but also discovered the local branch of the New York Public Library and devoured stories.

He continued to be an avid reader throughout his youth, even hiding in a tree at the park to read. But he did not find himself in the books he read. Because as a young teen he was confused about his encounters with race, he thought he would stop being an African American. He wanted to be something that was not "Negro" like the maid or janitor portrayed in the books he read. Instead, he decided he would be an intellectual, someone who read books. He also wrote, primarily poetry that imitated the British poets he studied in school. It was not until he was in his twenties when he read works by Langston Hughes and James

Baldwin that he felt he had permission to write about Harlem, where he had grown up.

Walter Dean Myers' contribution to the literature that illuminates the lives and history of African Americans is invaluable, and he writes about his people with affection and humor, along with great literary skill and a seriousness of purpose (Bishop 1997, 394). With teens often as the central characters in his stories, his works convey the strengths of extended black families, and the importance of close relationships and of trust and love among family and friends. His stories leave readers with powerful pictures of young people's personal growth as they experience the pressures of living on big city streets. Yet, his insight into what it means to be human crosses all racial and ethnic boundaries. He cares deeply about the young people who are treated as "the others," those who are not the good students in school, who are not the perfect children. To him, diversity means humanizing *all* peoples (Myers 2005b).

His Books in School Settings

Since 1982 I have been reading countless works of young adult literature, teaching graduate and undergraduate young adult literature courses, and visiting many middle and high school classrooms. In each school setting, regardless of the students' age or grade level, Walter Dean Myers' works always have a profound impact on readers. Yet, particularly when college students read *Fallen Angels* (1988a) and more recently *Monster* (1999b), they ask questions about using the books in their middle and high school classrooms when they become teachers. They express concerns about some of the language use and the difficult situations and issues in the books. They express surprise when I tell them that I know *Fallen Angels* is a book some high school students read on their own and that *Monster* is a favorite of many students in our local middle school.

At Dempsey Middle School in Delaware, Ohio, two eighth-grade teachers, Maggie Massaro and Judy Hollander, work with librarian Karen Hildebrand to plan and teach a unit on Walter Dean Myers, a unit that covers from three to eight weeks, depending on the year. It is a favorite unit for them and for their students, who first hear an overview about the author and his works and then choose books from an extensive class set and library collection. The goals for the unit focus on students enjoying and appreciating literature. They also learn about various genres of literature, participate in well-designed lessons that address many language arts standards, choose books for individual reading, listen to select works read aloud, produce informal and formal written works, take part in small group and whole class discussions, and complete a poetry project at the culmination of the unit. For this book, I observed the middle school classes, interviewed the librarian and two teachers, and collected a variety of instructional materials and student work samples. The first three chapters include information drawn from the work done in the middle school; however, ideas from the unit can be adapted to fit other grade levels, including high school settings.

Any book about teaching the works of Walter Dean Myers must include a chapter on *Fallen Angels* because of the significance of this novel, which has become for students and many teachers a work of historical fiction. In the middle school, one of the teachers permits her more mature readers to use this work as an individual choice book, but it is not used for whole class lessons. However, at a nearby high school in Powell, Ohio, Olentangy Liberty High School, English teacher Zana Adams teaches a unit she designed with librarian Kathy Orr. The central work of the unit, which focuses on the randomness and extremes of war, is *Fallen Angels*. Students learn about the Vietnam War and consider issues that compare and contrast with those of past wars and current situations. A second English teacher, Christopher Moore, also uses the book with his students whose reading of *Fallen Angels* begins with poetry and short stories as they probe ideas about war and heroes. Their reading of the novel leads to written work in various formats and culminates in a poetry–protest song project.

Book Overview

As a boy, the person who became Walter Dean Myers wanted to be good, but he didn't know where he fit in, so he rejected the value system that seemed unattainable. Today the multitudes of readers who admire his books find inspiration in the story of what occurred in his life between his youth and his many achievements in the literary world. Therefore, information about his life and how he became a writer is blended in each chapter of this book as it relates to his literary works. In addition, each chapter includes instructional ideas about how teachers use his books in classrooms and how students respond to them.

Chapter 1, "'I Was Not in the Books': Walter Dean Myers, the Man and His Works," includes highlights about the author's life, his early experiences, and his body of work, as introduced to the eighth-grade students by Karen Hildebrand, the middle school library media specialist. Her multimedia approach is the "kickoff" of the Walter Dean Myers Unit for students in the grade eight language art classes. Interspersed in this first chapter are images of the Harlem of Myers' youth as portrayed in his stories and poems, including the beautiful poetry collection *Here in Harlem: Poems in Many Voices* (2004b), and what he describes as his set of themes: father-son relationships, identity problems, aspects of human vulnerability as he understands them, and the values he hopes to bring to those who have not been valued. This chapter also includes an exploration of his memoir *Bad Boy* (2001b), of the novels *Handbook for Boys: A Novel* (2002a) and *Autobiography of My Dead Brother* (2005a), and of numerous works of nonfiction, including his picture books for older readers.

Although there is a consistency in his basic themes, Myers continues to expand the literary elements of his craft by exploring the possibilities of language and form. In each subsequent chapter, there is an elaboration of these literary elements in the many genres of his works and information about how teachers have used his works in various classrooms.

Chapter 2, "'I Tell Stories Too, Only I Write Mine Down': Stories in Many Genres," focuses on how middle school students come to know some of the many forms/genres of Myers' stories, primarily the short stories "The Treasure of Lemon Brown" (1983) and "Reverend Abbott and Those Bloodshot Eyes" (1996a). Students also explore the stunning visual and written images in his picture books, poetry, and the play *Cages* (1990a). These works speak powerfully about the many aspects of what it means to be human, as noted in students' written responses to the photos and poetry in *Brown Angels: An Album of Pictures and Verse* (1993a), *Glorious Angels: A Celebration of Children* (1995a), and *Angel to Angel: A Mother's Gift of Love* (1998b).

One of the goals of the Walter Dean Myers Unit is to give students the opportunity to learn about a variety of genres. The students read *One More River to Cross: An African American Photograph Album* (1995b) as an introduction to Myers' works of nonfiction, particularly the African American history that is an important part of his writing. Their study of *One More River to Cross* includes written work in which they explore the theme of the words and pictures of the book.

Chapter 3, "Life in Harlem: Choice Novels and Poetry," includes the favorite novels teachers select for whole class reading, especially Myers' first novel, *Fast Sam, Cool Clyde, and Stuff* (1975), and the students' self-selected books ranging from the humorous *The Young Landlords* (1979) to the realistic *The Beast* (2003a) and *Shooter* (2004d). Intertwined in the chapter is information about the written work and projects students produce based on their choice book, such as the novels *Slam!* (1996b), *Monster* (1999b), *Scorpions* (1988b), and various works of historical fiction. Using their choice book, students complete a poetry project as the culmination of the unit. This chapter concludes with a summary about how the unit matches various local and national academic content standards.

Chapter 4, "*Fallen Angels*: Young Adults and the Extremes of War," focuses on a high school unit that centers on *Fallen Angels*. In this novel, Myers expresses what he sees as the waste of war, the lies that are told about it, and how sanitized and glorified it is, particularly to young people. This powerful novel conveys that the real obscenity is not the language used by the soldiers but the war itself. When young people read *Fallen Angels,* they learn about the randomness of war and its long-lasting effects. This chapter includes information about how teachers provide background knowledge about Vietnam and address key facts and false ideas about the war, and how they use a variety of print and nonprint media for well-planned activities that occur as students read, write about, and discuss the novel. The activities and projects that extend students' understanding of the novel and the unit's theme include using related poetry and films. Students participate in multiple writing opportunities ranging from research papers on a chosen topic to essays that probe how a particular theme is developed throughout the novel. In an excellent culminating activity, students analyze poetic devices used in the lyrics of 1960s protest songs.

"Many Ways to Tell a Story: Three Remarkable Novels" is the title of Chapter 5. As Walter Dean Myers continues to expand his craft, the significance of the style and also the complex issues in *Monster, Shooter,* and *Street Love* (2006b) warrant special attention. In *Monster* Steve Harmon tells his story with his first-person handwritten memoir and his typed screenplay. The variety of surface effects such as drawings, photographs, mug shots, and video stills adds to the complexity of the social and racial issues raised in this multilayered, cinematic story. The style itself makes this novel worth exploring, and mature readers are aware of the intertextuality in *Monster,* which expands their appreciation of the artistry of Myers' literary works.

Myers is concerned about young people and what makes them violent. In *Shooter,* Myers shows that people who are outsiders look for others who are outsiders. In this book, pieces of the story are told in various print formats, including reports, newspaper articles, and diary entries. The story in *Street Love* is conveyed in free verse that is a blend of iambic pentameter and street language. It is another beautiful and touching example of the artistry of this award-winning author, his concern about young people, and his place as one of the most important writers of literature for young people.

"I Was Not in the Books"

Walter Dean Myers, the Man and His Works

Would a person with a speech impediment who dropped out of high school be someone who would speak to large audiences of teachers and librarians and say, "My reading takes me places my parents never saw"? or, "I write the best I can and let the audience find the book"? Or would he write, "My life has been one long adventure with language"? (Myers 2001a, 58) Could it be the same person who was expelled from school several times by the time he was in fifth grade? In less than an hour's time, eighth-grade students in one middle school not only find out the answers to these questions but also look through countless books and choose ones to check out and read. Their Walter Dean Myers Unit has begun. They learn about this versatile, talented, prolific author and his award-winning literary works of all genres. Before the unit ends, they will have the opportunity to read, write, and talk about stories as a whole class and with a small group of peers, and individually complete a poetry-story project with their choice novels.

As the unit begins, the students file in and find seats in a classroom that is part of the library media center where Karen Hildebrand begins the "Walter Dean Myers Kickoff." Tables around the perimeter of the room are filled with his books, grouped in categories. Karen's multimedia presentation is an introduction to "The Man Behind the Books," who, as she says, is well known now, but that was not always the case. She blends biographical information and various influences on Myers' writing with short, well-prepared book talks and pictures. By the time the class period ends, students know that Walter Milton Myers was born in 1937, one of eight children and the son of a coal miner. They learn about his adoption by the Dean family before he was three years old, which occurred after his biological mother died. Many years after his adoption, when Myers published his second book, he honored his foster parents, the Deans, by using the pen name Walter Dean Myers.

As Karen continues her introduction to the man and his books, students learn about Myers growing up in Harlem, the difficulties resulting from his speech impediment, the influence of the teacher who gave him "real stories to read," his attendance at a high school for gifted students, and his unattainable desire to go to college. They listen when Karen tells them about his skill as a basketball player, about the reason he became a "marked man" who left high school and joined the army, and about his education and the various jobs he had when he returned home. Students hear Myers' words on a short video clip (*Book Fair Magic* 1995) as he talks about the importance of literacy: "The only thing I had when I went out to fight the demons of the world was my reading." He tells the young people about his book *The Glory Field* (1994), his novel that traces the Lewis family for 250 years. He wants readers to think about his people's struggles as they tried to take control of their lives and determine their own destiny.

Myers often talks about the importance of one teacher who told him he could write. But young people are amazed that one man can write so many books and of such a wide variety of genres, beginning with the text for a book that won a prize in a contest for African American writers, the picture book *Where Does the Day Go?* (1969). At the time in his life when he wrote this book, he had resumed writing because he realized he was getting little satisfaction from his "outside" life. "The process of writing, the almost mystical act of putting marks on paper" continues to hold an enduring fascination for him (2001a, 61).

It is interesting for students to know about Myers' daily schedule, starting at 4:30 a.m., and about his approach to writing, which begins as he learns all he can about his characters and the situations of their story. On many occasions, Myers has talked and written about his process of writing a story (Myers 2001a, 2005b). He looks at a collage of photographs, put together by his wife and posted on the wall of his tiny writing room. The next step is to put them into story form. He believes that this process of transferring an owned character or idea into a new context is the essence of the creative process. The structure of most of his writing consists of six parts, beginning with the introduction of the characters and the conflict, followed by the character going through the easy stuff and applying the obvious logic to solving the problem. If the conflict ends here, there is no story. In the third part, the character realizes there are no easy answers, creating the crisis. The conflict must work within the confines of the story, but it doesn't always have to be an extension of the main character (www.authors4teens .com). The fourth part of the book involves the personal growth of the main character. It is through this growth and the insights the character attains that Myers reveals his intent in writing the story. The fifth part is the conclusion wherein he makes sure that the actions of his protagonist are instrumental in reaching the resolution. The story ends with the wrap-up. Along the way to the end of the novel, as he explains, he uses "the same techniques that I use as a reader. I use word symbols and language clues to convey my story" (2001a, 62).

In Myers' early works, including his first novel—the chapter that became a book, *Fast Sam, Cool Clyde, and Stuff*—themes begin to emerge that are important in his adolescent novels: the importance of the peer group, particularly when growing up;

father-son relationships; and African Americans helping each other. Most of the earlier novels are set in Harlem and avoid the harsher aspects of life, such as drugs and violence. Told with humor and authentic dialogue, these stories focus on what brings people together. Although there is universality to his themes, Rudine Sims Bishop explains in *Presenting Walter Dean Myers* (1991):

> his works offer an authentic portrayal of Black urban life. Within the context of a milieu that has the potential to destroy lives, Myers offers love and laughter, compassion and hope, and an emphasis on the spirit and resiliency that enable young people to survive. He also offers humor as a welcome antidote to potential despair. (ix)

Many of his works, complete with the sights, sounds, and smells of day-to-day life in Harlem, show the role of humor and the wisdom and insight that can help young people understand what it means to grow up Black in urban centers. As Bishop (1991) points out, "Racism is a given. Myers is also clear about the potential for overcoming the hardships. . . . He writes of the need to find strength with oneself and of the possibility of finding strength within the group. Whether the group is the family, the peer group, or the community" (96).

Harlem, Basketball, Gangs, and Choices

In the beautiful poetry collection *Here in Harlem: Poems in Many Voices* (2004b), Myers honors the Harlem of his childhood. He remembers the community of shops and markets reflecting a dozen different cultures, the churches, the absolutely charming brownstones, the wide streets, and the music he heard everywhere. He recalled reading *Spoon River Anthology* by Edgar Lee Masters in high school and "began to imagine a street corner in the Harlem of his youth and the very much alive people who would pass that corner. So began *Here in Harlem*" (2004b, viii). Every voice is based on someone he knew, from the deacon in the church to the laborer, from the jazz artist to the undertaker; and Clara Brown, the dancer-singer who offers her testimony throughout the book, has seen it all. The songs of his people are sometimes funny, sometimes sad, but they are his history and the core of his cultural roots. *Here in Harlem* includes many of his heroes, such as Langston Hughes, Countee Cullen, and Joe Louis. He added photographs to the text, not specifically to match each poem, but because he loves the images, and for him the images and the voices are "a sustained triumph of place and community" (2004b, viii).

In her unit kickoff, Karen Hildebrand embeds her talk with information about Harlem and about the many awards Myers has earned. She shows the students a book cover of what looks like graffiti. The words are actually the titles of his award-winning books. The book, *Handbook for Boys: A Novel* (2002a), is a story full of Myers' insight for teen boys as conveyed by Duke, a barber who is concerned about the kids in the neighborhood. Duke wants the young Black males to know they have choices about such things as whether they see the value of reading and choices when making decisions about sex and drugs. He emphasizes the importance of not thinking like a victim. Myers is concerned about why young people are so violent. "What is happening?" he asks. He often speaks about the fact that he does not believe in bad seed, that young people want to find value and be good. In his books, rather than explicitly telling teens what they should do, he discusses possible strategies for them to use in dealing with the dilemmas of life.

When Karen shows the basketball books—*Hoops* (1981), its sequel *The Outside Shot* (1984b), and *Slam!* (1996b)—it is clear these will be favorites of many students. The stories convey one of Myers' primary themes: even under difficult circumstances young people have choices and must take responsibility for their decisions. In *Hoops*, a more gritty story than other early ones such as *Fast Sam*, Lonnie wants to use basketball as a way out of poverty, but learns he needs more than basketball skills to succeed in life. Yet the dream is kept alive. In *The Outside Shot*, Lonnie faces new challenges during his freshman season at Montclare State, a small midwestern college, as he struggles to keep up academically, must continue to fight racism and corruption, and shows his compassion and sensitivity as he helps Eddie, a disturbed, withdrawn young boy. Lonnie is surprised to find out that his roommate Colin, who is white, is also poor. In all three basketball books, Myers uses a first-person narrative voice and the vernacular of the Black urban adolescent. The books are sports stories that also have much to say about survival and hope, friendship and family relationships, options in life, and the need for skills beyond basketball.

In *Slam!*, published fifteen years after *Hoops,* seventeen-year-old Greg "Slam" Harris focuses on his basketball skills instead of his poor grades at his new magnet school, a school for "smart" kids, most of whom are white. Like Lonnie, Slam dreams of playing professional basketball and making it big. He begins his story with great confidence: "Basketball is my thing. I can hoop. Case closed" (1). But his grandmother is very sick, his father has lost his job again, his best friend, Ice, seems to be dealing, he is not sure where he stands with his girlfriend Mtisha, and he can't understand how to do his math homework. He learns that it is not a weakness to accept help, that he must play as a member of the basketball team, not as a one-man show, and that his art project of filming his Harlem neighborhood has merit. Like *Hoops, Slam!* is about more than basketball. In both books, the young stars worry about the changes in behavior of a best friend, and they reluctantly accept advice from an assistant coach who plays a significant role in helping them grow.

In the short book talks that are a key part of her kickoff, Karen doesn't hesitate to tell about the books that convey darker stories, such as the ones that show what can happen when poor young people who feel powerless turn to drugs and guns. Again in the Newbery Honor book *Scorpions* (1988b), Myers' compassion is clear, his ear for dialogue is apparent, and his characters are memorable. Twelve-year-old Jamal Hicks must extricate himself from a difficult and destructive situation, and his friend Tito must return to Puerto Rico because of what happens. In this story, Myers moves away from the first-person narration used in his humorous novels, and he includes a scene from his own life: jumping out of a tree and showing a knife to confront a gang so they would leave a young kid alone.

As Karen does a brief talk about another Newbery Honor book, *Somewhere in the Darkness* (1992b), she shows editions of the book with three different covers and notes how the cover of a book can help a reader make some predictions about the story. In this book, Myers again shows the love of a member of an extended family and the challenges to achieving self-esteem. He also explores a type of conflict between fathers and sons; but the journey itself, when Jimmy's father, Crab, takes him halfway across the country, and Crab's difficulties with the law are the conflicts that propel the story. However, as in all good literature, the conflict works within the confines of the story.

Like Jamal in *Scorpions,* Jesse in a more recent book of fiction, *Autobiography of My Dead Brother* (2005a), likes to draw. Both boys use drawing to try to make sense of their life in Harlem, the challenges of their friendships, and the territorial conflicts of gangs wherein guns and drugs are a constant threat. *Autobiography,* a National Book Award Finalist, is a conventional novel about the teen artist, Jesse, who watches the deterioration of his close friend who is his blood brother Rise. Jesse uses his sketchbook and comic strips in an attempt to understand the changes occurring in Rise's behavior. The illustrations for the story of his friend are powerful black-and-white sketches drawn by Myers' son Christopher. The book, written with authentic street dialogue, conveys the territorial conflicts between Rise and the Diablos gang. The book begins and ends with "Precious Lord, Take My Hand" sung at another funeral for a teen whose life ends in violence.

The struggles of the characters in *Autobiography,* as they face various choices, show Walter Dean Myers' concern about young Blacks who are at the point of making life-changing decisions. He shows that even under the worst of circumstances, the characters do have choices. When interviewing teens in detention centers and jails, he has noted that they are the same individuals that a few years earlier were against drugs and crime. Myers wrote about *Autobiography* in an interview with Don Gallo: "I think the kids run into a reality wall that they can't get over. They need mentoring, stability, and a belief system that is modeled in the home, not just presented as an academic concept. Two kids, almost brothers, one has the modeling and the other doesn't, are the core of the book" (www.authors4teens.com 2003).

In another work of contemporary teen fiction, *The Dream Bearer* (2003c), twelve-year-old David meets the "dream bearer" Moses, an old man who is the voice of the civil rights movement. David depends on Moses, his mother, and his close friends, Sessi and Loren, to help him understand his father's outbursts and unstable behavior. The action in this book, like in many of Walter Dean Myers' stories, takes place on 145th and 147th streets in Harlem, a place full of vacant buildings and empty promises. *The Beast*, also published in 2003, is a novel in which there are two stories, one about Anthony "Spoon" Witherspoon who leaves Harlem to attend a prep school in Connecticut and the other about his girlfriend, Gabi. While Spoon is away at school, Gabi loses her foothold on life and is overtaken by the temptation of drugs, "The Beast."

More Genres

As she notes that Walter Dean Myers can "do it all," Karen continues with brief introductions to his works of historical fiction, including his books in the *Dear America* series and *The Righteous Revenge of Artemis Bonner* (1992a), a book that resulted from Myers' exploration of the history of black cowboys. She talks about nonfiction works such as *Now Is Your Time! The African American Struggle for Freedom* (1991b), *Amistad: A Long Road to Freedom* (1998a), and the intriguing *At Her Majesty's Request: An African Princess in Victorian England* (1999a), a book based on a group of letters by and about a little African girl who was brought to England in 1849. After Myers found the letters in a shop in London that specialized in antique paper items, he did extensive research to write what led to this intriguing book.

Karen shows the class a favorite of hers, the biography *Malcolm X: By Any Means Necessary* (1993b), and one of interest to many students, the biography *The Greatest: Muhammad Ali* (2001c). Noting that Myers' vivid memoir *Bad Boy* is really an autobiography, she explains that in this book readers learn more about the man behind the books. In it, Myers tells about his loving family, his school experiences filled with failures, the trouble resulting from life with some of his peers, and his love for reading and writing that ultimately brought him success and fulfillment.

Students learn of additional notable works of nonfiction, including *USS Constellation: Pride of the American Navy* (2004e) and *Antarctica: Journeys to the South Pole* (2004a), a book in which Myers explores the fascinating history of Antarctica. It includes old photographs and diaries and letters of the explorers, including Shackelton's crew who, stranded on the shore, wave to Shackelton and a small group who row off in the middle of nowhere to get help. In another work of nonfiction, *The Harlem Hellfighters: When Pride Met Courage* (2006), Myers and historian Bill Miles tell the story of the 369th Infantry Regiment, a group of Black soldiers who fought in World War I, men "who gave good accounts of themselves when so many people thought, even hoped, that they would fail" (149). The photographs in the book include scenes of these brave men on the battlefield and their triumphant parade in New York when they returned from the war.

Karen introduces picture books, some of particular interest to older readers: *The Blues of Flats Brown* (2000a), *Malcolm X: A Fire Burning Brightly* (2000b), *I've Seen the Promised Land: The Life of Dr. Martin Luther King, Jr.* (2004c), and *Patrol: An American Soldier in Vietnam* (2002b), the powerful story-poem with stunning collage illustrations. She shows the endpapers and talks briefly about the young soldier and what he faced in Vietnam.

Noting that blues music is a key part of African American

history, she shows students a book that explores the power of music and color, *Blues Journey* (2003b). In its illustrations, Christopher Myers uses the same blue ink, white paint, and brown paper bags on each page. Referring back to the jazz music students heard as they entered the room, Karen shows the students the beautiful book *Jazz* (2006a) with its amazing blending of words and pictures. The fifteen poems in *Jazz* reflect the sounds and colors of the various styles of the music, and the illustrations, also by Christopher Myers, make the rhythms visual. *Jazz* and *Blues Journey* are the stories of how this truly American music developed. In both books, Walter Dean Myers has included a section with historical information about the music.

Additional genres represented in Myers' work include his retelling of African folktales such as *The Dragon Takes a Wife* (1972), in which the Black fairy speaks in the street jargon of the day. A more recent book, *A Time to Love: Stories from the Old Testament* (2003d), is hard to classify: it's a picture book with brilliant illustrations by Christopher Myers, is a book of six short stories, and can be considered as nonfiction. The prologue was written by Michael Myers, a chaplain in the U.S. Air Force.

As a contrast to the way young readers expect a story to be told, they see the results of Myers' experimentation with narration as he uses various formats and fonts in *Monster* and *Shooter*, two powerful novels of realistic fiction for mature readers. "Was he guilty?" "Was not making a decision a bad decision?" Karen asks as she shows the full cover of *Monster* and talks about the awards and the writing style in the book, which has no pages of plain type. She points out the striking illustrations by Christopher Myers. From her brief book talk about *Monster*, students learn that Steve Harmon is in jail accused of a crime. Steve, who doesn't want to be seen as a monster, tells his story through his journal entries and the movie script he writes. In *Shooter*, a story with a suburban setting, Myers examines what drives young people to such desperate acts as school shootings. The construction of the book is interesting in that Myers uses reports about a school shooting and a question-and-answer format of interviews that various investigators conduct with two students, Cameron Porter and Carla Evans, whose answers show the different ways the characters perceive their lives and the impressions others have of them. The book includes a final report, journal entries written by another student, "Len" Leonard Gray, newspaper reports, and a medical examiner's report.

Karen ends her presentation with words about a humorous book, *The Young Landlords* (1979), a story about kids who buy a tenant apartment house for one dollar. In this book, published twenty years before *Monster*, Myers demonstrates his skill with language, particularly with the characters' word play, and his ability to blend humor with the underlying, more serious issues. In *Young Landlords*, he conveys genuine warmth for his characters, explores father and son relationships, and shows the importance of companionship to urban Black teens.

A young person on the video clip Karen shows to the students asked Walter Dean Myers for whom he writes. He responded, "Let the audience find the book." And most certainly those who make up his vast audience of readers of all ages have found the remarkable treasure of his books. And as the unit kickoff ends, students begin their discovery of the vast treasury he has created. They head to their classrooms with the books they have already chosen from the library, and their immersion into a wonderful unit of study is underway.

"I Tell Stories Too, Only I Write Mine Down"

Stories in Many Genres

Like his father and grandfather, who were both great oral storytellers, Walter Dean Myers is a teller of stories, but his are written down. "Whatever happens, don't stop writing, it's what you do," he recalls Ms. Liebow, his high school teacher, telling him. Writing is one thing for which he was praised in school, and writing is what he continues to love doing. And he knows what makes a good story. His father told him scary stories. His grandfather told "God's-gonna-get-you stories" based on the Old Testament ("The Young Adult Novel: Writing for Aliens" 1988c). As a boy, Myers did not like his grandfather's stories, but later realized that his grandfather was passing down to him the cultural substance of their people, of their lives—the ideas of moral being and judgment and of storytelling itself. As Myers states in "Cultural Substance: A Writer's Gift to Readers" (1991a), he feels strongly that a writer must bring to young people a history of the experiences and values that identify the writer's cultural being. For him that experience is a celebration of African

American life, a celebration that he conveys to readers in the form of many written genres in addition to his numerous books of fiction, nonfiction, historical fiction, short stories, plays, poetry, and picture books.

Myers often says that being raised Black in America has been the major influence on his life. But he first had to figure out whether being Black was a good or bad thing. "This is no mean trick when all of the heroes I was presented with were White," he wrote in a brief autobiographical sketch published in *Speaking for Ourselves* (Gallo 1990, 148–49). His discovery of Langston Hughes, who lived a few blocks away from him, led to his realization that he could write about poor people, particularly poor Black people. And he knew the value of story from his mother, who realized that reading stories can be a refuge for people who, like them, could not afford other things.

Stories, the Songs of His People

Myers' focus on the value of the stories of those who have gone before is stated so well by a nine-year-old boy in his beautiful short story "Jeremiah's Song" (1987b). Although his cousin Ellie said the stories were not true, the young narrator liked to hear them. "Grandpa Jeremiah said they wasn't stories anyway, they was songs" (194). "'You think on what those folks been through, and what they was feeling, and you add it up with what you been through and what you been feeling, then you got you something'" (200). As Grandpa Jeremiah is dying, he tells his grandson that the stories are a bridge and a meaning. "'Then when things get so hard you about to break, you can sneak across that bridge and see some folks who went before you and see how they didn't break. Some got bent and some got twisted and a few fell along the way, but they didn't break'" (200).

The pictures of some of these people who have gone before appear in a book that can be used as a wonderful beginning activity for a Walter Dean Myers Unit. *One More River to Cross: An African American Photograph Album* (1995b) is a story told through black-and-white pictures accompanied by Myers' poetic narrative. It is a beautiful portrait of the people of African descent in the United States: "It is not the only possible portrait, but it is one that I believe has not often been seen," Myers states in the introduction. In this stunning book, he has gathered pictures that show his people's struggles and accomplishments, their joy and sense of communion. There are pictures of religious services, music making, holiday celebrations, hard work, and happy young men and women. "Here are people being people, unburdened by the historical restrictions of race, defining themselves according to *their* understanding of who they are" (vi). The intimate photographs, many from his vast private collection of over 10,000 images, show the lives of Black Americans and the powerful journey they have undertaken over the last 150 years. An eloquent, simple narrative accompanies the photographs with words that emphasize hope, strength, endurance, victory, love and learning, and the depth of the human spirit. "And at the center of all were the families" (41). In the back of the book, Myers explains that not all of the photographs in the book can be accurately dated, but he includes the source of many of them. The important thing is that the images remain and the history must be reconstructed.

As an introduction to Myers' works of nonfiction about African American history, which is clearly an important part of his work, teachers Maggie Massaro and Judy Hollander have their students read *One More River to Cross* and write about its words and photographs. As a class, first they read the introduction together, and then, sharing the four copies available in the classroom, students silently complete the book. Their individual assignment is to find two pictures that are of particular interest to them. They write a description of the ones they have chosen and what it is in each image that has led to their selecting it. Using the accompanying words and the details about each image that are noted in the back of the book, they write what to them is the theme of each picture.

In her work with *One More River to Cross*, Jordan learned the meaning of vocabulary words: *confluence, communion, preconceptions, segregation,* and *adversity.* She summarized key points from the introduction by noting that there are as many similarities as there are differences between people of African descent in the United States and others. She pointed out that, regardless of the historical photographs, some people don't acknowledge what African Americans have done, including the important contributions they have made, such as fighting for our country. She described a photograph (117) that was especially meaningful to her:

> In this picture there are men, workers, and shopkeepers. They are standing around a radio as if they are listening to music. The men seem very cheerful and are smiling. Some look like they are tapping their feet or dancing. At the bottom of the picture, it says "Again we made do." I think this picture means that even through bad times African Americans still found enjoyment. I think it also shows that even if African Americans didn't have expensive things, sometimes simple things are much more enjoyable.

Jordan has conveyed in her work that this picture and Walter Dean Myers' carefully chosen words are not consistent with a distorted view of the lives of African Americans with its myth of under-achievement and stereotyping of Blacks as people who are restricted in ability and who have not participated in what this country has offered.

Myers' closing words in *One More River to Cross* make a powerful statement that applies to all of his work: "The story is of triumph and endurance and of the breadth and the depth of the human spirit. The reason for the story, for the celebration of what has been, is that the journey continues" (151). His accessible histories of African Americans, or Black Americans, a term he often uses, include *Now Is Your Time! The African American Struggle for Freedom* (1991b). In this book he combines history, biography, and some of his own genealogy. The historical content, told in a narrative format, enables students to understand key events from the early days of slavery to the civil rights movement. He explains the strife endured by generations of African Americans who have longed for freedom.

The stories of Myers' people are also told in numerous works of historical fiction. In the novel *The Glory Field* (1994), he follows one family from the forced voyage of enslaved Africans to America through to the present. The novel begins in 1753 when eleven-year-old Muhammad Bilal is captured off the coast of West Africa. The family story continues on a plantation, follows members of the Lewis family from South Carolina to Chicago, and ends in 1994 in Harlem, New York. Along the way various descendants escape and find Union soldiers, flee north to escape the Klan, work for a white family in Chicago, own a beauty business, play basketball, go to Vietnam, and settle in Harlem. One descendant, Malcolm, goes back to Curry Island, South Carolina, for a Lewis family reunion; is concerned about a cousin who uses drugs; and learns the Lewis land is to become a resort. Readers can trace the various people in the story by following the family tree pictured at the beginning of the book.

It is interesting for students to know that when he was writing *Now Is Your Time!*, Myers realized he wanted to know more about his own background. Using what he knew about his family and information from the U.S. Census Bureau, he learned that his great-great-great-grandmother was living on a slave-breeding plantation in Jefferson County, West Virginia, when the Civil War ended. Some of his people were still living on the same plantation. As noted in a short interview published in the March 26, 1993, issue of *Scholastic Scope* (Rinaldi), he feels that is important for African Americans to do research about their families and find out that their history is not all painful, that there might be wonderful things to discover.

Students who are interested in biographies seek out the stories Myers has written about various historical figures. His stories about Malcolm X are told in two separate texts: a chapter book, *Malcolm X: By Any Means Necessary*, and a more recent illustrated biography, *Malcolm X: A Fire Burning Brightly*. Myers depicts the adversity of a man who was an interesting figure of the civil rights era, but he also conveys Malcolm X's ability to move from hatred to tolerance. In *The Greatest* (2001c), his biography of Muhammad Ali, Myers explores what Ali meant to America and why there was so much interest in professional fighting, especially in light of Ali's physical difficulties. Whatever the genre in which Myers tells the stories of his people, they are filled with insight about the human experience for readers of all groups and ages.

Short Stories: Growing Up in Harlem

Myers' short stories are an important part of his large body of work. Through these stories, students learn something about what it was like to grow up in Harlem in the 1950s. As a boy, Myers focused on games like Scoop Ball or Kick the Can. He wasn't concerned about violence or about being poor. "When I was a kid in the late forties, I thought the whole world was like Harlem, full of life and colors and music that spilled out onto the streets for all the people to enjoy. Life was a constant adventure," and so begins the short story, "Reverend Abbott and Those Bloodshot Eyes" (1996a). These words set the stage for a humorous story about the "fight" between the kids and the visiting minister Reverend Abbott. The Reverend didn't realize the welterweight champion, Sugar Ray Robinson, wasn't really going to fight with the boys in the neighborhood. Part of the adventure of living on the block was that athletes such as Sugar Ray or Willie Mays either lived in Harlem or spent time there.

It was not the athletes who intimidated the kids. What they really had to worry about were the "Window Watchers," the women who would report to the mothers what they saw going on, and the "Root Ladies," who could give the evil eye to anyone who broke the "rules." One thing the Window Watchers and the Root Ladies liked was that the kids in the neighborhood attended Sunday school and played basketball in the gym at the Presbyterian Church, where there were even dances for the teenagers, which Reverend Abbott didn't seem to like. On a day

Reverend Abbott was to deliver a sermon in the morning and conduct a funeral in the afternoon that might be attended by gang-
sters, everyone was stunned to hear the song "OOOOOO-EE
Don't Roll Your Bloodshot Eyes at Me," instead of "What a Friend
We Have in Jesus," the usual hymn that was played over the sound
system on Sunday morning to summon everyone to church.

As part of the Walter Dean Myers Unit, the eighth-grade
teachers, Maggie and Judy, use the short stories "Reverend Abbott
and Those Bloodshot Eyes" and "The Treasure of Lemon Brown"
for lessons on comprehension, sequencing, vocabulary, character
study, and conflict. They choose to either read these stories aloud
or have students read them in small groups. In "The Treasure of
Lemon Brown," a story first published in *Boy's Life*, March 1983,
Greg Ridley's mood matches the dark, angry sky. He is tired of his
father's lectures about studying math to improve his grade if he
wants to play basketball. To escape the thunderstorm, he enters an
abandoned building and confronts an old, raggedy Black man who
was at one time "Sweet Lemon Brown." Greg learns about Lemon
Brown's treasure hidden under the man's rags—yellowed newspaper clippings and his battered harmonica—that was sent back to
him after his son Jesse was killed in the war. Lemon Brown
explains to Greg that he had given the clippings and harmonica to
his son: "I didn't have nothing to give him except these things that
told him who I was and what he come from. If you know your
pappy did something, you know you can do something too." This
short story is a good example of how, to Myers, fiction closely follows reality. It contains excellent examples of various kinds of
conflict: person versus person, self, nature, and society. Readers
understand the definitions of vocabulary words, such as *vaulted,
gnarled, ominous, octave, tentatively,* and *tenement,* from the context
of the story.

"The way I see it, things happen on 145th Street that don't
happen anywhere else in the world." So begins the delightful short
story "Big Joe's Funeral." It is one of the ten short stories in Walter
Dean Myers' collection *145th Street*, published in 2000. When
Maggie reads the story "The Streak" aloud to her students, it

becomes one of their favorites. They understand Jamie Farrell's feelings when he seems to have a long streak of bad luck. When students have completed their assignments for the Walter Dean Myers Unit, they often choose to read other short stories in this collection. With these stories, students are immersed in the vivid setting of the Harlem streets, the people who lived there, and Walter Dean Myers' skill as a storyteller. He remembers what it was like to grow up, and he knows about the problems faced by young Blacks in America today.

Walter Dean Myers' many short stories are published in a variety of collections and are excellent examples of contemporary realistic fiction. Many of these stories can be paired with specific books. For example, in Myers' story "Stranger" published in Don Gallo's collection *No Easy Answers* (1997c), Cassie Holliday feels that nobody cares, and she tries to ease her pain by taking "a little something." Soon she is horrified by the stranger she sees in the mirror. Gabi in the novel *The Beast*, like Cassie in "Stranger," is also overwhelmed by harsh realities and loses herself to drugs. Myers' story "Briefcase" in Harry Mazer's collection *Twelve Shots: Outstanding Short Stories About Guns* (1997a) reflects Myers' concern about the ready access of guns. The story leaves unanswered the question of whether the narrator, a bike messenger, will use a gun to avenge the man with the briefcase who, he thinks, has no respect for him. This story works well with the novels *Scorpion* and *Shooter*. The stories such as "Stranger" and "Briefcase" do not contain the humor of the earlier stories. They show the darker side of life in Harlem. Yet like Myers' other works, they clearly establish a sense of place and convey his compassion for young people.

Poetry: The Angels

As the unit study of various genres continues, students read some of Myers' beautiful poetry, wonderful examples of the songs of his people and of all humankind. Between 1993 and 1998, Myers published the three striking angel poetry books: *Brown Angels: An*

Album of Pictures and Verse; Glorious Angels: A Celebration of Children; and *Angel to Angel: A Mother's Gift of Love. Brown Angels* is a collection of turn-of-the-century photographs of African American children. Children from different heritages around the world are celebrated in *Glorious Angels,* in which each picture is accompanied by the words of a beautiful poem. In his introduction to this book, Myers writes, "Children remind us of those days when the world was a place of wonder and excitement, a time when love was freely given and play was a serious part of life. . . . When we celebrate these children we celebrate ourselves" (unpaged). In the third book, *Angel to Angel,* family bonds are celebrated. The images are reminiscent of the relationship Walter Dean Myers had with the woman who became his mother.

During the silent reading time that is part of the unit, the middle school students choose one of the angel poetry books to read and respond to in writing. They choose a picture they like or one of particular interest, describe it in detail—facial expressions, clothes, how the person is standing or sitting—and explain how they think the person feels. Their explanation includes what led to the idea about their feelings. They also choose a poem from the same book and explain what they like about it and the specifics about how it says what it does: the rhyme, rhythm, theme, feeling it evokes, and what it reminds them of. The work with the angel books can be either an assignment required for the whole class or an optional choice for extra credit. In either case, it gives the teacher another opportunity to show Myers' versatility and talk about the specific genre of the books.

The Play *Cages*

At any point when it fits in the unit, Maggie takes about three days for students to read *Cages,* a play written by Myers and published in Don Gallo's 1990 collection, *Center Stage: One-Act Plays for Teenage Readers and Actors.* The play is an excellent way for students to explore symbolism as they discuss what each character and object represents. In the play, each character—Oliver, Willie, John, Maria, Peggy, Ellen, and Yoshiro—stands in a cage he or she has created with chalk and is reluctant to leave. In small groups, students read various character parts, take notes on the characters, and discuss the play. They soon notice the significance of the cages, river, key, and crowd noise.

For their concluding activity, students work in groups with a large piece of colored paper on which they write their ideas about what the characters and the four objects represent. The cages appear to be a boundary of fear, a wall individuals have built around themselves. Maria is willing to take risks to get out of her cage; Willie, the only Black guy, is seen as a warrior but he is afraid and doesn't want to be a victim; Oliver agrees he too is not willing to take risks; in despair Yoshiro runs away; Peggy, like a guardian angel, makes a key for the others and tries to help but they are not willing to accept her help. Some students see the river as another boundary, an obstacle to overcome; others view it as a place of the death of aspects in one's life that die out when cleansed, as in baptism. To students, the crowd noise represents society in general in which characters are afraid of the real world. Maria is the only one to hear laughter; the others cannot see pleasure. Students decide that individuals must be comfortable with themselves to leave their cages. The whole class discussion concludes with their responses to two questions: How did Maria feel at the end of the play? What would the characters such as Ellen and John be like in the real world?

Although *Cages* is written in a different format from Myers' other works, it too is an engaging story with memorable characters and much to think about. Middle school teachers, Maggie and Judy, who teach the Walter Dean Myers Unit focus first on students' enjoyment of all the literature, their engagement in the stories, and their various responses to them. As students explore their interpretations, whether individually, in small groups, or as a part of a whole class, they have many opportunities to represent and expand on their ideas about the nonfiction, historical fiction, short stories, and poetry. The teachers' reading aloud of Myers' works and students' silent reading of their choice novels continue throughout the unit as other activities—such as their work with the angel poetry books and the reading of the play—take place, all with the central focus on their author study of Walter Dean Myers.

Life in Harlem
Choice Novels and Poetry

The journey to Harlem "started on the banks of the Niger and has not ended." With these words, readers of the book *Harlem: A Poem* (1997b) join Walter Dean Myers as he takes his son Christopher on a trip back to the Harlem he remembers. The result is Myers' beautiful poem with pictures by Christopher in which the words and striking illustrations of collage art connect readers to the music, art, literature, and everyday life of Harlem, a neighborhood that was home to famous athletes and to artists, a place where Langston Hughes, Countee Cullen, and James Baldwin lived. It is also the place that becomes the home of Fast Sam, Jamal Hicks, Richie Perry, Steve Harmon, and all the other characters Walter Dean Myers brings to life in his books.

It is important to Myers to transmit his ideas and feelings using the rich cultural tools of his Black heritage. In his article "Writing for the Uninspired Reader" (2005d), he states that if he does not succeed, the failing lies with him as much as with the reader: "Writing, for me, becomes most satisfying when it is the openly complicit and joyful act of a writer and reader both enjoying a book" (38). When Walter Dean Myers writes, he is aware of the *uninspired reader* (a term he prefers to *reluctant reader*). To him the key question is whether reading is pleasurable instead of being a chore and, therefore, another opportunity for young people to fail. He relishes the experiences he shares with inner-city youth and writes using the "rich cultural tools of his heritage." He wants to bring all readers to language and to convince them that the journey through story is worthwhile. To ease them through the entire experience, he is careful to define the language he is using in the first chapters of a book.

Because of his artistry as an author, the details of his characters' lives become meaningful even to those who do not share the specific experiences. His books not only reach readers who understand the culture and subculture of the setting from which the words and situations are derived; they also have a universal appeal. This wide attraction is apparent when students have an opportunity to select from his extensive list of novels to determine which one will be their choice book as the focus for a variety of activities and projects during their participation in the Walter Dean Myers Unit.

Happiness and Friendship

In his early novels, Walter Dean Myers creates characters, portrays situations, and conveys themes that can be traced throughout all of his work, whether fiction or nonfiction. As he notes in the introduction to *One More River to Cross*, life includes struggles and difficulties, but it is also full of the happiness that comes from being part of a caring family and having the support of a group of friends. Life also presents opportunities for making choices and for noting the accomplishments and contributions of others.

In *Fast Sam, Cool Clyde, and Stuff*, first published in 1975, Myers re-creates the Harlem neighborhood he remembers. Relationships with teenage companions are essential in this episodic novel, which began as a short story. As Rudine Sims Bishop points out on *Presenting Walter Dean Myers* (1991), he is keenly aware of the potential for destruction and despair among urban Black youth. Yet he also knows about the love and laughter that are an important part of friendships as the young people sit on the stoop and talk with each other, as they challenge each other to ball games, and as they offer each other support. With this first novel, Myers' talent as a writer was recognized: his keen ear for dialogue, his creation of believable, likable characters, and his ability to write humorously even when the underlying themes are serious. In *Fast Sam*, as in his other early novels, *Mojo and the Russians* (1977), *The Young Landlords* (1979), and *Won't Know Till I Get There* (1982), Myers treats his characters with empathy and affection, has a good sense of drama, and keeps the stories moving. Some of the darker realities of living in the city are key parts of his third novel, *It Ain't All for Nothin'* (1978), a story in which twelve-year-old Tippy must live with his father, a petty thief who drinks and smokes weed. As Bishop points out, "The books are humorous, but with the humor they also address some serious issues and themes—death, drugs, sex, family relationships, individual and group responsibility" (1991, 18).

Fast Sam is an excellent choice for reading aloud to students, which Maggie Massaro does during the Walter Dean Myers Unit. She finds it to be a wonderful book for discussion because of the many issues raised in the story and also the opportunity for laughter. Even though there are episodes in the book in which the teens get in trouble with the police, they do not commit any crimes. They are the "116th Street Good People," an interracial group of teens who care about protecting each other, "not from fighting and that kind of thing, but just from being alone when things get messed up" (1975, 74). Stuff, who tells the story and whose real name is Francis, is twelve and a half, bright, and sensitive; gets scared and cries easily; and laughs at himself. He and his friends, especially Fast Sam, Cool Clyde, and Gloria, are memorable and well-rounded characters.

In *Fast Sam*, as in other early novels, the girls are strong characters, the boys try to figure out their relationships with their fathers, and their natural-sounding dialogue shows Myers' use of the grammar, semantics, and rhetorical styles of Black English vernacular (Bishop 1991, 36–37). In the narrative, there are examples of boasting, signifying, verbal performances or raps, and the use of call-response patterns. The characters are, therefore, recognized as genuine reflections of young people growing up in a Black cultural setting. But they are also recognized as a part of families with the values of the American middle class: their fathers want their sons to better themselves, their mothers care about them, and they are expected to take advantage of opportunities their parents did not have. They are young people who see themselves as positive and upbeat, and the appeal of their stories is not limited to African American readers.

In *Won't Know Till I Get There*, Myers weaves together two themes: relationships within a family and intergenerational conflicts. Stephen, who is fourteen years old, has difficulty getting along with Earl, the troubled foster child his parents have invited into their home. When Stephen, Earl, and two friends are caught spray painting graffiti, they are assigned to work at a home for seniors. It takes time for the feisty seniors, whose home is being closed, to accept the teenagers and their help. Although there are several humorous situations in this story, there are also disturbing realities. The teens are disappointed about how callous the social agencies are, and the seniors do not all find a satisfactory place to live where they can stay together.

Survival and Decisions

Myers' stories, in which the urban reality is more than backdrop, also reflect his memory of growing up in Harlem and his ability to create ordinary people living in sometimes desperate circumstances. Drugs, poverty, and violence have a more prominent role in his stories of realistic fiction than simply being part of the setting. An overarching theme, as exemplified in *Scorpions*, published in 1988, is that survival, both psychological and physical, is possible even in very difficult situations, and young people have options about the decisions they make. Jamal tries to juggle his role as student, son, and brother as he is pressured by his jailed older brother's gang, the Scorpions, to become the leader and take part in the gang's activities. The choice between peer pressure and family is a difficult one for Jamal.

Regardless of the setting or family situation, Myers celebrates the spirit and strength of those who survive and make the right choices. *Crystal* (1987a) is the story of a beautiful sixteen-year-old model exploited by some adults in her life and supported by others, primarily her father and an elderly neighbor. Poverty is not a problem for Crystal, but she must choose between the pressures of modeling and what she must do to maintain her integrity. Even without the optimism of the earlier stories, Myers conveys compassion for the characters in *Crystal* and in his later books, such as *The Beast, Handbook for Boys, Monster,* and *Autobiography of My Dead Brother.* Although the behavior of the young people might be questionable, his hope for their survival and growth is evident.

Choice Novels

Students know from the beginning of the unit when librarian Karen Hildebrand does the author study kickoff that they will select one of Walter Dean Myers' fiction or nonfiction books to read as their choice novel. The books are all on display around the room, and many students choose multiple novels to read during the three weeks they have to complete their reading of the stories. However, they all decide which one book will be the focus of various written responses in which they demonstrate their interpretations and critiques of the book.

The variety of favorite novels chosen by students includes *Monster, Scorpions, Won't Know Till I Get There, Slam!, Shooter,* and *Fallen Angels.* Some of the strong readers choose *The Glory Field.* Maggie talks individually to students who choose to read *Fallen Angels* to be sure they will not be uncomfortable with the language used by the soldiers. She feels it is important to determine whether they are mature enough to handle the violence of the war and the novel's dialogue. While other students are reading their choice novels during silent reading time, a special education teacher reads *The Mouse Rap* (1990b) to inclusion students. In this story, each chapter begins with a rap. Mouse is fourteen and, like so many of Myers' protagonists, he lives in Harlem, loves basketball, and is part of a mixed cast of characters who are of various ages and socicultural groups. Students enjoy this story about Mouse and his friends, who work together to solve a mystery about some missing loot from a 1930s bank heist.

 Writing Activities

During Reading

When Maggie and Judy assign written work to be completed while students are reading their choice novels, they provide specific directions that include various options. Judy suggests students take notes as they determine the main conflict in the story, with details about when it starts and which characters or situations are involved. Her students also note details about the ending of the story, specifically how the conflict is resolved and whether or not they would change the ending. They also either draw or use magazine pictures to show three scenes from the book with a written summary explaining the pictures. These scenes can be either humorous or disturbing, but the description is to be sufficient for someone who has not read the book to understand the events.

Maggie's assignment for journal entries, to be written as students read, includes the requirement that there must be at least four lengthy journal entries that are "organized, detailed, and well written." Students choose the specific topics of the entries about their novel from a list. Maggie emphasizes that students use supporting details and examples from the book. The list includes many choices about what aspects are to be the focus of their four written entries: a character and his or her role in the story, the main events of the plot, the dilemma or problem the main character is dealing with in the story, a scene that is especially funny or one that was troublesome, a situation in the book that the student relates to and details about how it was handled, or a character that is similar to a real person and the differences from and similarities to that person. Students can also decide to write as a critic stating specific reasons and details supporting why they either like or dislike the book (Figure 3–1). Or students can choose a day when they read "a fair amount" of the book and describe in detail what they have read and their feelings about that portion of the story.

After Reading: Lit Letter

After Judy's students hear Karen's introduction to Walter Dean Myers and his works, they make a folder to keep all their papers related to the unit. These papers include their notes about the author's life, their responses to *One More River to Cross* and to the short stories read in class, and their description of the pictures from the angel poetry books (as discussed in Chapter 2). The students also keep information about what they will write in their four-paragraph "Lit Letter," in which they tell the addressee about their novel. Judy gives them a specific format so they also learn about letter writing.

Lena's letter about her choice novel begins with information about the main characters:

> One dilemma that Jimmy, the main character in the book, *Somewhere in the Darkness*, has is that he is torn between the only home he has always had and the father he had always wanted. . . . Jimmy decides to go with Crab and soon finds out that his decision will take him to interesting places and uncover some untold secrets along the way.

Lena explains what bothered her: "Jimmy had to quickly make his decision and either decision he made would hurt someone." Noting that she does not usually read books of this type and that Myers "put the characters in situations that were strange" and disturbing to her, she would recommend the book to others.

The following journal entries must be written about your chosen novel, NOT *Fast Sam, Cool Clyde, and Stuff.* In order to assess your understanding of the book, you must make four (4) journal entries that are *organized, detailed, and well written.* Choose your topics from the list below. Make sure you identify the number of the choice you are writing about. These should be lengthy accounts, at least three quarters of a page each.

Journal Topics

1. Choose a character and describe the character's role in the novel. Pull information from your reading and give examples to support your ideas about this character.
2. Describe the plot of the novel. Use characters' names and specific situations from the story to detail what the novel is about. Be sure you tell the main events from beginning to end.
3. Describe the dilemma or problem the main character is dealing with in the story. Be sure to give specific details.
4. Have you ever found yourself in any situation similar to that of the characters in the book? Describe your situation and how it relates to the situation in the book. How did you handle it?
5. Describe a scene from the book that made you laugh. Give specific details from the scene and explain why it was funny to you.
6. Describe a scene from the book that bothered you or made you sad. Give specific details from the scene and explain why it troubled you.
7. Identify a character that reminds you of a real person. Describe the similarities and differences that you see between this real person and the character in the book.
8. Be a critic. Tell me what you liked and disliked about the book. Support your opinions with specific reasons and details from the book.

FIGURE 3–1. *Author Study—Walter Dean Myers*

After Reading: Persuasive Essay

One possible extension of the Walter Dean Myers Unit is to have students write a persuasive essay about their chosen book. Before they begin writing, they are to decide whether they would like to either persuade others to read the book or persuade them *not* to read it. They must have at least three supporting reasons for their decision about the book and at least two examples from the book to support each reason. Maggie reminds them to be sure they do not get "FRIED," because they have not included facts, reasons, incidents, examples, and details. They understand what she means by "SESWADWWAP" (start each sentence with a different way within a paragraph). A large display on the wall includes examples of various ways to begin sentences so students learn about sentence variety. Their essay must follow a specific structure and make a strong case for why the student would or would not recommend the book to another reader. These essays lead to an opportunity for extended instruction about various genres and about writing conventions, in addition to discussion about the stories.

When teaching the students about an effective persuasive essay, Maggie talks about using transitions at the beginning of each paragraph to help the flow of the essay. She uses terms such as *dependent clauses* and *prepositional phrases* so the students learn about grammatical terms in context, and she reminds them about the required bibliographical citations. To support the students' completion of a successful essay, Maggie provides a "persuasive essay checklist." Before students turn in the final draft of the essay, they must respond to the checklist questions. It helps them to look back at their own writing to be sure they have fulfilled the assignments and adhered to expected writing conventions.

Poetry Project Extension

As the unit comes to a close and students have finished reading their choice novels, they complete the poetry project. As with the unit kickoff, the librarian again has a key role. After Maggie introduces the project, Karen talks about some of the seventy poetry books she has brought to the classroom on her poetry cart. She shows the students examples of poems that relate to the various works of Walter Dean Myers. For example, a book of cowboy poetry connects to a favorite book, *The Righteous Revenge of Artemis Bonner*, set in the 1880s, in which Artemis heads from New York City to the Arizona Territory and turns cowboy avenger. Mel Glenn's *Back to Class* (1988) shows a way to write a poem about a specific character. Several collections, such as ones about a journey or father and sons, relate to *Somewhere in the Darkness*. The poem "The Block" by Langston Hughes (1995), a favorite poet of Myers', captures the setting of Harlem. Maya Angelou's poem "Life Doesn't Frighten Me" (1993) connects to *Scorpions*. Karen reads Nikki Giovanni's "The Drum" (1985) and explains that after Myers came home from the army and had no direction, he shifted around and played the bongo drum. Even though he later found his own rhythm, his father was not happy with his drifting.

To help students look for poem-story connections, Karen suggests, as listed on her handout, that they think about characters, settings, relationships, friends, parents, school, plots, themes, emotions, diversity, minor characters/people, inner city, brothers and sisters, writing, genres, and more. She shows them the artwork done by street artists and the color in some of the books. Karen gives the class a variety of ideas and shows them the poetry books she used when she chose one specific poem as her connection to *Slam!*.

To complete the poetry project, although they are encouraged to find more, students find at least ten poems with a connection to their chosen Walter Dean Myers' book. On a prepared sheet, they record each poem's title, the poet's name, the title of the book in which the poem is published, the page number, and the connection to the story. This exercise leads to students' exploration of a variety of books and types of poetry. They then select one poem to complete the project by displaying it on a poster of their own design. The poster includes a copy of the chosen poem; a clearly written explanation of how, in at least three ways, their novel and poem connect; and attractive decorations related to the novel and/or the poem (Figure 3–2). To complete the poster, students must think in

You must find at least ten (10) poems that have a connection with the novel you chose to read by Walter Dean Myers. If you find more than ten, each counts as one point extra credit. You can find up to thirty (30) poems. From this collection of poems, you must choose *one* to use for your project.

For the project, you must make a poster. The poster needs to include *a copy of the chosen poem, a written explanation of how your novel connects to your poem,* and *attractive decorations related to your novel and/or your poem.* The poem you choose does not have to be found in a book. You can create your own poem to connect to your novel.

The explanation of the connection must be clearly written. Specifically identify lines from the poem and detail how these lines connect with specific things that happen in your book. When looking for connections, keep these things in mind: characters, settings, relationships, friends, parents, school, plots, themes, emotions, minor characters/people, inner city, diversity, brothers and sisters, writing, children, genre, or other thoughts.

FIGURE 3–2. *Walter Dean Myers Poetry Project*

ways far more challenging that writing a book report as they make decisions about images that relate to key events, colors that fit the tone of the story, words that represent a character's feelings, and the best way to write about how specific words or phrases expressed in the poem connect to particular aspects in the book.

For her poetry-story connection, one girl composed her own poem to express her ideas about *Motown and Didi: A Love Story* (1984a). Another student, Lolita, used Maya Angelou's poem "Grey Day" (1994) to represent her ideas about *At Her Majesty's Request: An African Princess in Victorian England.* Lolita explained how the poem connected to Sarah's sadness when she was moved away from her people in Africa, the differences between the normal dress of the two cultures, and the queen's "lonely heart" eased by Sarah's presence. Lolita decorated her poster with the vivid colors of purple, dark pink, and green to frame her pictures of beautiful Black women. She added to her poster key words she had cut out from magazine pages—*life, mother, African, blood, rule,* and *beautiful.*

The tone of the poster James created for *Monster* is somber with large gray lines to represent jail bars and blue and gray lettering surrounded by cut-out pictures: a black male, two monsters, and a policeman arresting a young person. James' drawing of a book with the title "The Life of Steve Harmon: Movie Script" is purposely placed behind the jail bars. In his explanation, James focuses on key words related to the story, such as *nightmare, scary and cold,* and *locked away.* James explains, "Steve thinks he will never get out of jail because he says[,] and other people say[,] he is a monster." It is clear that the vivid images from Myers' novel have conveyed to James the chaos, fear, and uncertainty of Steve's life in jail and his despair as he awaits the court's verdict.

Another student's choice of color also showed his careful thought about what would best fit a particular story. Luke's pictures, selected poem, and written explanation are pasted on red poster paper, an appropriate color to fit the blood shed by the soldiers whose story is told in *Fallen Angels.* Luke found multiple lines in the poem "A Grateful Heart" by Nancy Meek (2001) that relate to Perry's experience in Vietnam. Luke's explanation includes specific events from the novel:

> The war was on a foreign land (Vietnam), and Perry stared death face-to-face many times. The time he stared his own death in the face was when a Vietnamese soldier held him at gunpoint, but luckily his gun didn't work. Another time he stared death in the face was when his friend Jenkins blew up after stepping on a mine. Perry was right there when it happened and right there when Jenkins died.

Luke noted that Perry, a combat soldier, "saw his time in hell with the death, destruction, pain, torment," and being shot while on patrol.

This project is an appropriate conclusion to a unit about the works of a literary artist who began writing poems as a child and who read and devoured stories. Walter Dean Myers had access to the world, to places his parents could never go, because he could read and assimilate information. To him, reading for everyone is the entry into the fullness of society. He told his audience at the 1988 ALAN Breakfast that nothing has been of more value to him than the reading of stories. "Ultimately, what I want to do with my writing is to make connections—to touch the lives of my characters and, through them, those of my readers." He would be pleased to know that when students complete the unit, they want to know what else he has written, and they continue to check his books out of the library. He has expanded their world.

The Unit and Academic Standards

The Walter Dean Myers Unit is a favorite unit for the teachers, librarian, and students at Dempsey Middle School. In addition to enjoying wonderful stories, becoming acquainted with an important author, and learning more about themselves and others, the young people develop many skills that connect to district and state academic content standards. The literature is the means by which they engage in a rich variety of language arts experiences. According to teacher Maggie Massaro, during this unit students learn about various genres and explore the grammatical structures chosen to tell a story. They learn about prepositions, run-on sentences and fragments, dependent clauses, and punctuation, such as comma rules. They explore literary devices such as symbolism and literal versus figurative language. They learn about the elements of literature: characters, plot, conflict, setting, pace, action, climax, point of view, theme, foreshadowing, flashback, mood, and tone. They develop the reading comprehension skills of predicting, questioning, recalling, summarizing, drawing conclusions, and engaging in self-monitoring during independent reading. To respond to literal, inferential, evaluative, and synthesizing questions, students engage in critical thinking at various levels. During portfolio conferences, they evaluate the processes of writing and look at what will lead to future improvement.

There are various kinds of assessments throughout the course of the unit, including oral responses during small group, student-to-teacher, and whole class discussions. What students have learned is also assessed with teacher-created worksheets, quizzes, and a test in which students apply their knowledge of the literal and figurative meanings of words and symbols. Their written assessments are both informal writing, such as the journal entries, and formal writing that culminates in the persuasive essay, a key assessment at the end of the unit. This finished product results from the recursive processes of prewriting, drafting, revising, editing, and finally publishing. In addition to decisions about word choice and sentence structure, as students work on their essays, Maggie builds in lessons on the structure of paragraphs and on syntax and the mechanics of language, such as spelling conventions, parts of speech, appropriate verb tenses, and regular/irregular verb conjugations.

The poetry project is not only an excellent extension of the unit but also another assessment. Students' responses to the literary works, both the novel and the poetry, must be organized in a way that shows an insightful interpretation with clear ideas and images that are specific references supporting the decisions about the choice of a poem's connections to the texts and conveyed in a polished piece of writing. In the course of making decisions that result in the finished posters, students must engage in critical thinking and use a variety of language arts skills.

Throughout the Walter Dean Myers Unit, students read and write a wide variety of literary texts; learn grammar and usage by studying how language functions in context; work with teachers and peers as a community of learners who are readers and writers; experience the interactions of reading, writing, speaking, listening, viewing, and representing as meaningful, communicative acts; have their work assessed by a variety of means; and share and display their own products. These language arts practices support important overarching goals: the opportunity for students to develop and apply strategies to comprehend and interpret diverse texts as they see a new view of their own world and demonstrate what they have learned about experiences they share with others.

Fallen Angels
Young Adults and the Extremes of War

To my brother, Thomas Wayne "Sonny" Myers, whose dream of adding beauty to this world through his humanity and his art ended in Vietnam on May 7, 1968.

Walter Dean Myers' dedication at the beginning of *Fallen Angels* (1988a) is a powerful statement about the tragedy of the Vietnam War, about all wars. He takes a strong stance about the need for young people to know what war is really like: "Teenagers grow up to be decision-makers. They grow up to be people who send others off to war. They . . . make decisions about war, often without ever really knowing about it, without understanding what it truly is." Myers spoke these words when he was part of a panel of authors whose topic at the 2005 Assembly on Literature for Adolescents (ALAN) Workshop was "Caring About Books on War." Others on the panel included Marc Aronson, Paul Fleischman, Harry Mazer, and Jim Murphy, authors whose fiction and nonfiction books about various wars are also appropriate for young people.

Myers told the audience that he had joined the army when he was seventeen. He was attracted to war as a teen and relished the idea of possibly getting into some sort of battle. His younger brother (Thomas Wayne), who had wanted to be an artist, saw Walter in uniform, followed his example, was sent to combat, and was killed in Vietnam. Myers speaks eloquently about how young men are interested in war, but television gives only a sanitized version, and the military says it has plans that will work, but "war is *chaotic.*" "Who is going to tell the children the truth about war *if not authors*? Who?" Myers asks (Aronson et al., 2006, 44). He answers this important and timely question: it is the authors whose works help young people think about this reality in their lives. Myers wrote *Fallen Angels,* based on his brother's death in Vietnam, and *Patrol: An American Soldier in Vietnam,* based on a friend's experience in the war.

Myers admits that he has two conflicting emotions concerning violence and war. In writing about war and his book *Fallen Angels,* he states,

> There is the same sense of excitement that I reach when I participate in sports, or even chess. I relish the idea of competition and even go so far as to romanticize it somewhat, even now. But I've seen dead bodies, and smelled decaying flesh, and none of it is romantic. I do feel a sense of guilt about my brother. (www.authors4teens .com 2003)

Walter Dean Myers' book *Fallen Angels*, set in Vietnam, presents war as it really is: painful, intense, terrifying, and without mercy. This compelling story is noted for its complex characters, genuine dialogue, vivid imagery, and figurative language, including the extended metaphor that contrasts war's realities with the romanticized portrayal in movies and on television. The story is told in first person by seventeen-year-old Richie Perry, who wants to get out of Harlem. He enlists in the army, although he, like Walter Dean Myers, is a bright, young man who wants to be a writer and attend college, but cannot afford it. Despite a knee injury that should have kept him from combat, Perry is sent to Vietnam in 1967; there he experiences his passage to adulthood. In *Fallen Angels,* Perry recounts the story of his soldier friends, especially Peewee, the high school dropout from Chicago who provides much-needed humor amid the intensity and horror. Perry tells about the prejudice they encounter, the "hours of boredom, seconds of terror" (132), and what it is like at age seventeen to participate in the realities of war and death. The violence in the story is controlled—it grows out of the setting—and the dialogue and language choices are authentic. It can be said that the real obscenity was the war itself, not the words the soldiers used.

The Vietnam War has been called "the living room war" because it was the first war viewed on television. Yet the experiences of the young soldiers, sent off to fight in a confusing jungle even before they were old enough to vote, were different from those conveyed in distorted media images. The soldiers entered the war as naïve young people, struggled to understand the war and themselves, and were transformed by their experiences (Johannessen 1993, 48). Many of them, like Walter Dean Myers, were underprivileged young men who thought the military would offer them educational opportunities and a source of income (Bishop 1991, 82). From his time in the army, Myers learned lessons about killing, about how a soldier must dehumanize the enemy. Because his high test scores pushed him into technical training, which he hated, he ended up training others to fight in Vietnam (www.authors4teens .com 2003). "The enemy was depersonalized by the use of a single pejorative term. The North Vietnamese were simply called 'gooks.' Focusing on gooks instead of people made it easier to think about killing them" (Myers 2001a, 61). Although Myers uses some of his own experiences in the story, he did not fight in Vietnam—the story is not an autobiography. As Rudine Sims Bishop (1991) points out, "*Fallen Angels* is a testament to his craft as a creator of realistic fiction. The book is a graphic and sometimes horrifying depiction of the waste, the futility, and the anguish of war" (83). Although it does not condemn or glorify the war, it leads readers to think about its complexities and consequences.

Because this book is as much about Richie Perry's coming of age as it is about the war, it is appropriate to use in high school classrooms. It has the structure of a romantic quest, an adventure story, but the similarity to romance ends with the story's circular journey. Sadly, the issues raised in the book are very timely. In addition, this well-crafted literary work can be used to help students deepen their understanding of many literary elements and the role these elements play in a well-told story. Because *Fallen Angels* is about an integrated group of Vietnam soldiers whose biggest challenge is pulling together for their mutual survival, it is an excellent choice as the central piece in a unit exploring the extremes of war or when studying the topic of war and looking at how various people respond to it.

The Extremes of War

Preparation for Reading Fallen Angels

Ironically, young people know more about earlier wars such as the Civil War than this more recent one, a war with legacies that still haunt us and with far too many parallels to current situations and tragedies. Larry Johannessen, a Vietnam veteran who became a high school teacher after returning from the war, points out in his publications that students lack knowledge about the Vietnam War. Francis Kazemek, who agrees with Johannessen, asserts that the impact of the Vietnam War is "felt daily in the lives of aging veterans, and their families. It is also felt in national politics and international diplomacy . . ." (1998, 156). Yet high school students, their teachers, and college students preparing to become teachers know little about the causes, events, and consequences of the war.

In his article "When History Talks Back: Teaching Nonfiction Literature of the Vietnam War," Johannessen (2002) explains why the topic is appropriate for mature high school students: it was a "teenage" war. Because the average age of soldiers was nineteen, they were not prepared for the carnage and terror of the Vietnam experience. In a year and a half, these idealistic men and women became disillusioned. In both his book *Illumination Rounds* (1992) and the 2002 article in *English Journal*, Johannessen identifies the stages of the experience:

1. The Mystique of Preinduction or the John Wayne Syndrome

2. The Initiation into the Military Culture in Recruit Training

3. The Dislocation of Arrival in Vietnam—Culture Shock

4. The Confrontation with Mortality in the First Firefight

5. Experience and Consideration: Confronting the moral dilemma; from innocence to experience and consideration; or from innocence to numbness and madness

6. The Phenomenon of Coming Home: How to live with the legacies of the war, with the guilt, the loss of faith, the loss of innocence

7. Putting It Together: Finding a Central Meaning.

As students read Richie Perry's story in *Fallen Angels*, they note how what Perry and his comrades experience compares to these stages as they change from being idealistic young soldiers to becoming men who must learn to live with the legacies of the war.

There are many ways for teachers to provide students with background knowledge about the Vietnam War before they begin reading *Fallen Angels*. The book *Patrol: An American Soldier in Vietnam* (2002b) by Walter Dean Myers is a stunning picture book appropriate for older readers. Myers' words and the collages by Ann Grifalconi capture the essence of U.S. involvement in the war: the soldier's fear, confusion, and thoughts about the invisible enemy, the jungle, and the people in the villages. There are no explicit descriptions of violence in the book, but it is a provocative story that sets the stage for reading *Fallen Angels*.

One high school teacher, Zana Adams, uses a video clip from Peter Jennings' multi-episode documentary *The Century: America's*

Time (1999) to prepare her students for reading *Fallen Angels*. Specifically, she uses the segment about Vietnam from the portion of the documentary that deals with wars America lost. With the class, she addresses both the false ideas and the facts about the war. Prior to the specific preparation for reading *Fallen Angels*, her students have read selected short stories and poetry from World War II. They discuss subjective and objective reporting about Hiroshima, do a quick-write about various political points of view, talk about the fact that some people say the Holocaust never happened, and complete a photo journalism activity.

To prepare his eleventh-grade students for reading *Fallen Angels*, Christopher Moore also uses selected poetry, short stories, and visual media. He reads out loud the poem "War Is Kind" by Stephen Crane (1899) and the song lyrics "Over There" by George M. Cohan (1917). His students compare and contrast the perspectives of the two poems in a journal entry in which they use as many words as they can think of to fill in the blank, "war is. . . ." After hearing the poems and considering their words, students write down two adjectives for each poem and describe the tone of each one. Students' ideas then lead to whole class discussion. To investigate the concept of heroism, students read short stories from their literature anthology. Stephen Crane's story "A Mystery of Heroism" (1898) leads to a discussion about whether or not the protagonist is a hero. After reading Ernest Hemingway's "Soldier's Home" (1925), a story about a soldier who returns home to Nebraska, they talk about an antihero.

To provide students with background knowledge and something to visualize, particularly with reluctant readers and visual learners, Chris also uses portions about Vietnam in Peter Jennings' *The Century* and clips from the Mel Gibson movie *We Were Soldiers* (2002). Students use prepared questions about the film *We Were Soldiers* to complete an in-class writing assignment. They consider how the battle of Ia Drang affects the soldiers and the American war effort as a whole, how the North Vietnamese are portrayed in the film, who shows the most bravery, and what point the film seems to make about the journalists who interview Colonel Moore after the war as contrasted with the man who was taking pictures during the battle.

In one essay written in class as a response to *We Were Soldiers,* Kathy wrote about how the Vietnam War transformed the young soldiers "into killing war-machines."

> At first . . . most of the men in the battalion are pretty much happy, normal men. They laugh and joke around with each other, and they are naïve to what the war will be like because they are young. Once they get to the battlefield, they find themselves doing just about everything to fight for their lives. . . . [T]he men begin fighting with their hands. They are so desperate to stay alive and so quickly used to the gore of war that they lunge at the Vietnam soldiers and kill them any way possible.

Kathy pointed out the way the film shows the loss of innocence and the shock resulting from what a helicopter pilot sees as he takes the wounded back to camp, and "he is enraged." She wrote about how quickly the eyes of a confident and spunky reporter are opened, and how he shuts down because of his fear and anger: "At one point during the battle, he no longer seems to care whether he lives or dies. He picks up his camera and takes pictures of all the atrocities; he doesn't even flinch. By the time that the battle has ended and the other more naïve reporters have landed, even his face looks different." Such observations show that students are ready to read *Fallen Angels.* As they talk about what they are reading in the novel, they continue to compare scenes from the documentary and the film with events in the book.

Character Development, Plot Conflicts, and Figurative Language
"Are these guys black?" students in one of Zana's classes wonder. They identify with the characters before considering race, a testament to Myers' ability to create characters who are credible young people even when the story's setting and situation are very different from anything the students have experienced. According to these same students, the language use in the story is not a problem

for them as they read, because they realize the word choice and dialogue fit the story. They also know the value of friendship, such as what Perry and Peewee, who is a favorite character of many readers, experience from the time they meet on the plane when flying to Vietnam. Adolescents understand what it is like to have doubts and questions, such as those of the young soldiers who must bond together if they are to survive all the dangers and uncertainties of the war. They know what it is like to look at themselves and try to figure out who they are.

As students read the book, they record responses in their reading journals, which are also referred to as logs. In addition to requiring students to pick one question from a general list of reading log starters, such as "When I started reading this book, I thought . . . , "or "If I could talk to [character's name], I would say . . . ," Chris and Zana pose a variety of questions for individual written responses that lead to small group and/or whole class discussion:

- How does the American military (as an institution) come off in the first two chapters? Find quotations and examples.

- Find quotations and examples that explain Peewee's and Perry's reasons for joining the military. Do you agree with the decisions they made and the reasons behind their decisions? Why or why not?

- What attitudes does Perry show about his future in this war? How do other soldiers feel about the future of the war? Find quotations and examples to support your point. What do Perry's assumptions show us about his character? Predict how his situation will end.

- What can we infer from the meeting between Perry and Judy Duncan? Support with details.

- Which character(s) so far best shows the "John Wayne Mystique"? Support with specific examples.

After students have read the first five chapters, they meet in small groups and talk about their favorite and least favorite character. With a reminder to use the terms *direct* and *indirect characterization*, they look at how they come to know the members of the squad. As students support their answers with specific words and actions from the text, they learn about Myers' approaches to character development, and they can make predictions about events that will follow.

Students also write down examples of various conflicts in the story, conflicts that occur in addition to fighting against the Vietcong and North Vietnamese: conflicts within the squad, those resulting from prejudice, conflicts against nature, and internal conflicts. As their reading continues, students consider how Perry's flashbacks enhance their understanding of the novel, what in the story surprises them, and what events indicate the "randomness of war," such as mistakes Perry makes and lives through. A vivid example of the horror of unexpected events occurs in a village the squad is sent to secure. Instead they find it burning and full of dead and injured civilians. The Vietcong (VC) had gotten there first. Perry enters what he thinks is an empty hut and would have been shot, but the VC's gun does not go off. Perry sprays the VC with bullets and again is horrified that he can kill. As he thinks about what he has done, he questions the purpose of the war, saying that trying to stop communism or stuff like that is different from shooting somebody. "It was different than being scared and looking at somebody who was maybe as scared as you were" (189).

Images and Ironies of War

In at least fourteen places in *Fallen Angels,* Myers makes comparisons to movies or television. One member of the squad, Lobel, whose uncle is a filmmaker, copes with the war by making it into a mental movie, until later when he kills his first enemy soldier and it becomes real. He keeps up a running commentary on how to make unnatural things look *almost* natural. He talks about what role they should each play, saying he could be playing the part of the baby-faced virgin who gets killed. Perry says he had thought Lobel was playing Lee Marvin and asks him if he doesn't know what role he is playing. Lobel is not sure, maybe a bad guy riding into town in a cowboy movie. He tells Perry, who is also not sure what his role is, not to be "the good black guy who everybody thinks is a coward and then gets killed saving everybody else" (76). When Perry writes letters home to his mother and little brother, he worries about what to say about the war. Perry doesn't want Kenny to think war is like the movies, yet writing about the realities of what he is experiencing would cause his mother to worry too much.

Vivid scenes stay with readers, such as the short clips that crowd Perry's mind when he can't sleep: "A few seconds of a medic putting a tag on a wounded soldier. A few seconds of a chopper taking off over the trees. A guy cradling a rifle. A body bag" (106). The stopping and starting of firing in the jungle battle seems as though someone is changing the channels and then switches back to war. During an intense battle late in the story, when Peewee moves toward Vietnamese voices, Perry does not want to move: "I wanted to sit there forever. Where the hell was the popcorn machine? Couldn't I just watch the rest of this damned movie?" (259).

An activity that works at any point in the reading, and it is one of the ways to probe the vivid word pictures and sounds in the story, is to have individual students write (or draw) in their reading logs a predominant image left in their minds, then to pose a question or issue they want to discuss that is connected to the image. Having students exchange logs, read what a peer has written, and write a response to it is good preparation for thoughtful whole class discussion, particularly as students consider the reality of the war images in the novel contrasted with war as portrayed by Hollywood and the media.

In journal responses and class discussion, students comment about how the "John Wayneism" illusion does not fit the reality of war. Myers' well-chosen metaphors are vivid and effective: the helicopters are

> Great insects, angry and buzzing over the steaming jungle, ignoring the fact that every hostile in the area was trying to bring them down. . . . The chopper crews. They were the stuff of heroes.

> Swooping from the skies like great heavenly birds gathering the
> angels who had fallen below. (183)

The term *fallen angels* (as in "all the angels warriors that fall" [44],
beginning with Private Jenkins) is a gripping metaphor for the
characters in the book, even those who return home and are no
longer the same people as when they left for the war.

The ironies in the novel add to the impact of the story. There
are excellent examples of dramatic and situational irony even in the
first five chapters. Teachers can guide students to find examples of
situational irony, such as the soldiers thinking they are safe
because they are less than a hundred yards from camp. But Jenkins
steps on a mine and is killed, a shard of metal protruding from his
chest. There are multiple examples of dramatic irony, such as the
missing paperwork that was to show Richie Perry should have
been exempt from combat because of a knee injury and the fact
that the soldiers think the war will soon end and they will be back
home.

Poetry-Story Connections

At any point before, during, or after reading *Fallen Angels*, students'
understanding about the war, and also of the literary craft of the
story, is deepened when connections are made with well-chosen
poetry. The poetry-story connections can be about tone, events,
themes, issues, setting, and even words a character could have spo-
ken, written, or experienced. Students learn with and from each
other as they articulate their ideas about the connections and listen
to what peers find as the links between the poems and the novel.
Finding the intersection between the texts enriches their understanding of both the story and the poems. For example, *From Both
Sides Now: The Poetry of the Vietnam War and Its Aftermath* (1998),
edited by Phillip Mahony, is collection of powerful poems written
by Vietnamese and American poets, both veterans and civilians.
The poems are arranged chronologically to correspond with the
progression of the war. Mahony states in his introduction that the
legacy of the Vietnam War is all around us, yet we seem "all too
willing to put that chapter in our history behind us" (9–10).

When students are asked why the teacher or another student has chosen a particular poem as a link, it leads them back into the story as they discuss various connections. As her students read and discuss *Fallen Angels*, Zana asks questions about why she chose to read a particular poem from Mahony's collection. Students realize that W. D. Ehrhart's "Guerrilla War" (1998b, 61) includes words that fit what the soldiers—Perry, Peewee, and their comrades Monaco, Lobel, Brunner, Johnson, and the others—experience because they can't tell the civilians from the Vietcong. After Private Jenkins' death, the soldiers realize the uncertainty of what might occur with the next step they take, as conveyed in Ehrhart's poem "The Next Step" (1998c, 57). It is interesting to note that Ehrhart fought in Vietnam and later became active in Vietnam Veterans Against the War.

As the story progresses, students might be asked to think about what kinds of death occurred in "Nam," to make a quick list, and then to listen to another poem in Mahony's collection: "Dead" by Mark Kessinger (1998, 118). They can also make predictions about what it will be like for Perry and Peewee if and when they return home, a question that will be answered when they read the end of *Fallen Angels*. Because of the examples in the story of Perry's concern about what to write in letters to his brother and his well-chosen words in letters to the parents of soldiers who died, students know he is a writer. What might he write in a poem about the experience of returning home? What will it be like? After they take on the voice of Perry and write about a soldier arriving home in the United States, they appreciate Ehrhart's poem "Coming Home" (1998a, 206), also in Mahony's collection. It speaks powerfully of what it was like for many soldiers.

Activities and Extensions

The War That Never Seems to Go Away: Doubts,
Questions, and Comparisons
The Vietnam question "Why are we in the war?" and the related question about when it will end are ones that Perry and his com-

rades ask, as did many people back home. Because it dragged on for more than a decade and cost at least 50,000 lives, it has been referred to as America's longest war. Questions about it keep returning. In an activity that engages students in critical thinking, Zana uses a *Newsweek* article by Evan and colleagues, "A Quagmire . . . in the Making? The Vietnam Question," published April 19, 2004. The article includes a subtitle: "In Iraq, the scale is smaller, but there are echoes. How it compares with Vietnam—and doesn't" (24). There are disturbing parallels: the desert in Iraq can be as confusing and deadly as the Vietnamese jungle is to Perry and his comrades; again it seems that America does not understand the enemy, and the conflict appears to be an open-ended war for vague or shifting reasons.

As students read the article, questions, including the following, guide their thinking as they compare and contrast the two wars:

- After reading the first paragraph, describe the tone (the writer's attitude toward the subject). Write down words, phrases, and expressions that demonstrate this tone.

- According to the author, why does President George W. Bush need to fear becoming like Lyndon Johnson?

- What does the *Newsweek* poll show about Americans' opinions about Iraq? (The article states that most are very concerned that Iraq will become another Vietnam.)

- What possible crisis does George W. Bush face that Jimmy Carter faced with Iran?

- "Vietnam is a recurring nightmare." How is Iraq similar?

- What is one significant difference between Vietnam and Iraq?

- What parallels might be drawn between the two wars?

- Why is the question of adding "boots on the ground" another debate that lingers from the 1960s?

- Why are American leaders divided over "The bigger the better?"

- How was the Iraq conflict supposed to erase all the ghosts of the Vietnam War?

- Explain how Vietnam and Iraq were wars of choice.

- What is one main difference between the Vietcong and Al Qaeda?

On the board, Zana records some key ideas of comparisons that emerge during the whole class discussion that follows the reading of the article:

Vietnam	Iraq
Guerilla war in jungle and civil war	Guerilla war in urban settings
To end communism	Against dictatorship and terrorism
"Make love not war"	"Make peace not war"
Protests against war	Protests against the war

Students realize the relevance of Perry's words from *Fallen Angels*: "I didn't want it to be real, this much death, this much dying, this waste of human life" (177). They consider terms used for various wars: World War II—*Good War*, Vietnam—*Bad War*, Gulf—*Fast War*, and Iraq—*Uncertain War*.

Zana concludes this activity with questions that build on the class discussion and the students' previous viewing of the movie *Forrest Gump*. In the movie they noted Forrest's focus on Vietnam and his observations of the country's reaction to it. Because students living through the Iraq war are observing the country's reaction to it, she asks them to think about their reactions to the two wars. "Do you see similarities, differences, or does it make a difference? Speak out. These are your thoughts."

More Movie/Book Comparisons
Using various media resources, including well-chosen movie clips,

is certainly appropriate with *Fallen Angels* because of all the comparisons to movies and television that are woven throughout the story. All or selected portions of the movie *We Were Soldiers* or *Forrest Gump* work as preparation for reading *Fallen Angels* or as part of the concluding discussion.

Chris uses the movie *Forrest Gump* with *Fallen Angels* for a compare/contrast activity. In his study guide called "The Vietnam Experience," he directs students to use his prepared questions as they take notes during the movie clip. After the viewing, the students are directed to construct responses that are clear and insightful using *specific details* from *both* the movie and the book:

- Compare and contrast reasons why each young man (Forrest, Bubba, and Richie Perry) decides to join the army. What do you notice about the circumstances in which each makes the decision to enlist?

- Compare and contrast Perry and Peewee's arrival in Vietnam to Forrest and Bubba's arrival in Vietnam.

- Compare and contrast the way soldiers in the movie cope with injury and death versus the way soldiers in the novel cope with injury and death.

- Compare and contrast the tone of EITHER the *Forrest Gump* clip and *Fallen Angels* OR the *Forrest Gump* clip and *We Were Soldiers*. Make sure you identify the tone and *how it is achieved* (this means specific details).

- Note one other comparison or connection between *Forrest Gump* and *Fallen Angels*. Your connection should be insightful and make reference to specific details from each source.

- BONUS: Identify one example of situational irony in the movie clip and explain it.

Such well-designed activities build on students' responses to and interpretations of both the visual media and the novel. They gain experience not only in doing comparisons and contrasts but also in

> What are some of the things that have surprised or shocked you as you read *Fallen Angels?*
>
> Explain what surprised or shocked you. What are some reasons for a soldier to fight and kill? Would you have reacted differently than the characters did? If you were not surprised or shocked, why not? Have you ever read a novel or seen a film that described what war is like? If not, do you have any reason for avoiding books or films about war? Explain the reasons why you feel the way you do.

FIGURE 4–1. Fallen Angels *Writing Prompt*

analyzing various media; synthesizing their ideas; formulating, supporting, and articulating their thoughts in oral and written formats; and learning from each other.

Writing Activities

A book as riveting as *Fallen Angels* can lead to multiple writing opportunities while students are reading the story and also for extended assignments. One of Zana's writing prompts leads students to think about what has surprised or shocked them as they read *Fallen Angels* (Figure 4–1).

When the students reach the second half of the book, Chris asks them to individually brainstorm two themes from the story and pick one to share with the class. He first gives them an example of a theme that fits *Fallen Angels*—loss of innocence—and the story's specific scenes that support the theme. In the whole class discussion that follows, students have generated many themes, which clearly demonstrate the depth of this novel: war as solution?, randomness/unpredictability of war, good and evil, coping with death, religion in war, loss of humanity, "The Enemy," heroism/antiheroism, responsibility and sacrifice, sadness and heartbreak, racism, boredom versus terror, the media in war, reality versus illusion in war, and the politics of war.

The theme essay assignment that follows the discussion begins with students first completing a prewriting piece in their journals as they respond to the following prompt: "Based on the evidence in the book, what *point* does Myers seem to be making about your chosen theme topic? Develop your response in depth with at least five sentences." Figure 4–2 shows the essay organizer Chris designed for students to use to find evidence to support their chosen theme. In the finished essay, due a week later, students analyze a chosen theme, tracing it in both plot and character development, making sure to clarify how the theme is developed from the beginning to the end of the novel. Based on the prepared rubric for the essay, students know they are expected to integrate quoted textual support in their analysis.

In her theme essay, Kathy probed the question about whether war is a solution and what fighting accomplishes:

> The violence and devastation felt on both sides is so great that it leaves everyone with the unanswered question: Why they were fighting? . . . The point that Myers ultimately illustrates is that war isn't a beneficial solution to a problem. He shows this through the change in the soldiers, the protagonist's questions to the meaning of war, and the ultimate outcome of Vietnam.

Kathy notes that the soldiers have different answers when asked why they are in the war because they do not really know why. It is not until Perry sees his first dead Vietnamese soldier that he begins to question the war, noting that they had cared for Jenkins who died because he had been one of them. "But the dead Vietnamese soldier, his body sprawled out in the mud, was no longer a human being. He was a trophy" (85). Perry wondered if he could become a trophy. Kathy wrote about Perry's thoughts about the meaning of war as his journey comes to an end. When trying to explain it to his brother Kenny, all Perry could say is that war is about killing. An example of the textual support Kathy chose to support her theme and its development through *Fallen Angels* is a powerful quotation from Perry: "I had thought this war was right, but it was only right from a distance" (269). The theme essay is an excellent example of a writing activity that helps students think about the unit topic,

List the theme topic you are writing your essay on: _____

Find evidence of your theme topic in EACH section of the book and list below. You will not use ALL of this evidence in your essay, but list everything you can think of now. You will decide what to use later. *Make sure to include page numbers for future reference.*

Section 1—New to War (pages 3–69)
Plot:

Character Development:

Section 2—Near Chu Lai (pages 70–128)
Plot:

Character Development:

Section 3—Angels Fall (pages 129–188)
Plot:

Character Development:

Section 4—Tam Ky (pages 189–252)
Plot:

Character Development:

Section 5—Song Nha Ngu River (pages 253–309)
Plot:

Character Development:

Based on the evidence you have found, write a thesis statement for your chosen theme topic. Remember, your thesis statement needs to tell what *point* the book seems to be making about your chosen theme topic.

Thesis Statement: _____

_____

Go back through the evidence you found and STAR the examples you have that will make the strongest argument. When you are finished, write three topic sentences (for each body paragraph) below.

FIGURE 4–2. Fallen Angels *Prewriting: Essay Organizer*

consider their interpretations of a piece of literature, and make decisions about how to convey their ideas in a polished piece of writing.

Another approach Zana uses that leads to a finished essay is the result of a research topic related to extreme situations or beliefs in recent wars. The specific topic is chosen by the student and approved by the teacher. Finding information for the essay can include an electronic research component for which students use a prepared chart to evaluate approved websites as they also note whether the information on each site is relevant to their topic. Librarian Kathy Orr offers support to students as they work on the electronic research. They use a research checklist and an essay planning sheet to document their work and guide their process, recording what they learn about both their chosen topic and the electronic information sources. As they write their essays, Zana builds in lessons about the process of researching a topic, organizing the topic into a finished product, developing a thesis with supporting statements and conclusion, and using specific bibliographic formats.

Because she knows the value of guiding students to look back at what they have accomplished, Zana gives them a freewriting prompt when the research assignment is completed. She asks them to think about their researching—including evaluation of Web resources, writing—developing a thesis with supporting statements and conclusion, and learning about topics related to extreme situations or beliefs in recent wars. Using what they have considered about their researching, writing, and learning, students explain in writing what they would do differently another time, or if they wouldn't change anything, why not. They use the prompt: "I used to think ... but now I think ... because. ... " In the process of completing the essay assignment, the students have an opportunity to meet multiple content standards related to research and writing.

Poetry Unit–Protest Song Lyric Project: A Culminating Activity
One example of an excellent culminating activity, assigned when students have completed the reading of *Fallen Angels*, is the Poetry

Unit–Protest Song Lyric Project designed by Chris. Students, with a partner or in a small group, are to create a poster that analyzes the *message, tone, figures of speech,* and *sound devices* in a 1960s-era protest song. Their requirement sheet includes information about how the final poster will be graded and what it must include: title of song and artist; copy of song lyrics; explanations of the literary elements of the song, such as figures of speech and how they are used; sound devices and how they contribute to the effect; the tone and what word choices and images create the tone; the song's theme or deeper meaning beyond the literal level of the lyrics; and a response to the song, in the form of a quality illustration or freewritten piece by each group member, that conveys his or her interpretation. Chris includes on the back of the assignment sheet a literary device definition page with a list of figures of speech and sound devices.

Before they work on the poster project, students work in class with a partner to complete a protest poem analysis practice sheet with Bob Dylan's "Blowin' in the Wind." They mark figures of speech and sound devices on the song's lyrics sheet and write down ideas about what the song means to them, along with specific lines that seem especially important. They closely examine two figures of speech and two sound devices and write about how each contributes to the song's meaning and effect (Figure 4–3). This in-class experience is a model of what they will do as they continue with the project.

For the poster project, Chris provides a list of songs from which students choose the one to use for their project, or they may find one of their own to analyze if it has school-appropriate lyrics and is approved by Chris. His list includes eleven songs, such as "Gimme Shelter" by the Rolling Stones, "Fortunate Son" by Credence Clearwater Revival, Janis Ian's "Society's Child," and "Ball of Confusion (That's What the World Is Now)" by the Temptations. The chosen songs include a variety of protest issues from the time of the Vietnam War. As students work on the project, they use a poetry project checklist (Figure 4–4) with reminders about what to write in their individual journals before meeting in

1. What do you think the song means (this needs to be MUCH more specific than just "it's against war" or "it's against racism"). Include any specific lines that seem important to you. *Hint: What do you think Dylan means when he says, "the answer is blowing in the wind"? What is he saying about the answer to his questions?*

2. Look more closely at two (2) examples of *figures of speech*. Identify and explain them below, especially how they contribute to the meaning of the song.
   In each case, point out:
   - *the line from the lyrics*
   - *what device it is*
   - *how it contributes to the song's meaning.*

3. Look more closely at two (2) examples of *sound devices*. Identify and explain them below, especially how they contribute to the song's effect on the reader/listener.
   In each case, point out:
   - *the line from the lyrics*
   - *what device it is*
   - *how it contributes to the song's meaning.*

4. Give an adjective that describes the *tone* of the lyrics. Explain how the author of the lyrics creates that tone with specific examples from the lyrics.

FIGURE 4–3. *"Blowin' in the Wind" Practice Sheet*

groups and what to do in the group sessions that must conclude with a decision about what each member is responsible for accomplishing before the next day.

The presentation of the posters completes a unit that began as students considered the tone of selected poems read aloud. The Protest Song Lyric Project is an excellent way for students to learn more about poetic terms, such as *hyperbole, simile, personification,* and other figures of speech, and sound devices such as *onomatopoeia* and *alliteration.* At the same time, they also see how the protest songs of the 1960s relate to *Fallen Angels* and connect to

1. Individual journal. Do this before you meet in groups.
   a. What do you think this song means? Get much more specific than "it's against _____." Write a brief paragraph that analyzes its message.
   b. Write one line you do not understand. What specific question do you have about this line?
   c. Describe the picture this song creates in your head when you read the lyrics.
2. Meet in groups. Perform the following steps.
   _____ a. In your group, share each member's responses to the above questions. Discuss specific lines.
   _____ b. As a group, circle and identify ALL figures of speech and sound devices in your lyrics. *Remember, a list is on the back of the assignment handout.*
   _____ c. Brainstorm your ideas for the song's tone. Underline specific examples of words and or phrases in the song that *best* illustrate the tone.
   _____ d. MOST IMPORTANT STEP—make sure you do this even if you do not get through all the above steps:

   Create an assignment for each group member tonight (typing blurbs, drawing your illustration, writing a paragraph, etc.). Write each group member's name and what he/she will be accountable for tomorrow.

   Name: Assignment:

   Name: Assignment:

   Name: Assignment:

Posters are *due at the end of the period Friday,* so make sure everybody has something to do.
More important, make sure everybody does it!

FIGURE 4–4. *Poetry Project Checklist*

what they have learned about the Vietnam War and various reactions to it.

Curricular Goals and Content Standards

When writing about the craft of *Fallen Angels*, Bishop (1991) notes how the elements that make Myers' writing commendable come together in this book: memorable, complex characters; genuine dialogue that defines the characters; dramatic descriptions with imagery and figurative language that paint vivid pictures of the setting, action, and characters; linguistic and situational humor; and a first-person narrator that keeps the reader close to the actions and emotions of the characters (84–85). Perry, Peewee, and their comrades certainly become real people that readers care about as they also expand their understanding about the randomness and extremes of war. As students write and talk about this compelling story, their responses and interpretations lead to multiple opportunities to note the many literary elements Myers used.

Both Zana and Chris know about the value of teaching *Fallen Angels*. Although, as Chris noted, because it is a long book particularly for reluctant readers, he gives students guidance with journal prompts, group discussion guides, and in-class reading time. At the same time, he found students reading who had previously been resistant to reading and writing. Some students read ahead, and Chris found one young man (who had not completed reading assignments all year) reading *Fallen Angels* during other instructional time. A highlight of the whole unit occurred when another student, who had struggled throughout the school year, spoke in front of the class for ten minutes. He voluntarily showed pictures of his dad, a Vietnam veteran who had died from complications from Agent Orange, and photos of the platoon with which he served. This incident is a moving example of how the Vietnam War continues to affect so many people and the value of teaching *Fallen Angels*.

As Rudine Sims Bishop (1991) states so well, "*Fallen Angels* is a powerful evocation of the Vietnam War and an indictment of war in general. It recognizes and celebrates the bonding that grows from shared experiences. It also recognizes that young men who face the conditions of war also face themselves" (91). It is a book that reminds us that war provides angel warriors, men and women, lessons in how to kill in order to stay alive; but some become the fallen angels. "The survivors have other lessons to learn. Having learned to kill, having learned to face death, they come home to relearn what it means to be an ordinary human being" (92).

Many Ways to Tell a Story
Three Remarkable Novels

The more I write the more I lean toward expanding the craft elements of my profession....I write about father-son relationships, identity problems, and aspects of human vulnerability as I understand them....But by exploring the possibilities of language and form and using the craft as a point of entry into the work, I can maintain my own vital interest in the themes and present at least what appears to be a wider menu. (www.authors4teens.com 2003)

Expanding His Craft

Walter Dean Myers' exploration of new possibilities of language and form is particularly evident in three novels that are the focus of this chapter. Young people who read any of Walter Dean Myers' literary works know that he is a gifted storyteller. When they read his award-winning novel *Monster*, published in 1999, or the 2004 publication *Shooter*, or *Street Love*, published in 2006, they also see what can be done when an author finds new ways of telling the stories.

The suburban setting of *Shooter* varies from the streets of Harlem, where the other stories take place. Yet in all three books of contemporary realistic fiction, Myers tells gripping stories using a variety of formats as he continues to expand the artistry of his craft. At the same time, he continues to probe questions about identity and individuals' self-concept, the influence of history and culture on identity, the effects of crime on the family of the accused, and the complex aspects of human vulnerability.

Myers understands the realities of growing up in urban settings, but he also admires people who take responsibility for their own lives. Because of his compassion for young people and his concerns about how they choose to live, he seeks answers to important questions. He wonders why some teens are so violent. What drives young people to make the decisions they do? What competing social, legal, and moral forces are part of their stories? These questions are certainly raised in his novel *Monster*.

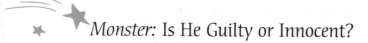

Monster: Is He Guilty or Innocent?

In *Monster* there are two juries who decide whether Steve Harmon is guilty or innocent: the one in the courtroom and the one that is reading Steve's story. *Monster* is a multilayered and multitextual book that is a favorite choice book for many middle school readers and is one that stuns college English majors with its intensity, artistry, and complexities. This highly acclaimed novel was the first winner of the Michael L. Printz Award, a National Book Award Finalist, a Coretta Scott King Honor Book, and a *Boston Globe–Horn Book* Honor Book. From the powerful and frightening image of the first sentence, "The best time to cry is at night" (1), readers are immersed with Steve Harmon in the fear and desperation of being in prison. They are left hearing what Steve hears, remembering what he says, seeing the powerful images that are part of his story, and pondering answers to many questions. Steve's handwritten journal entries and his neatly typed screenplay of the courtroom proceedings, which he calls "A Steve Harmon Film" (277), tell the story. A variety of surface effects, such as drawings, photographs, mug shots, and video stills, adds to the impact of the story. Readers hear and view what is happening as directed by Steve, who includes cinematic cues such as fade out, cut to, CU (close-up), VO (voice-over), LS (long shot), and POV (point of view).

The story takes place in a New York City correctional facility and the streets of contemporary Harlem. Sixteen-year-old Steve is Black, scared, and alone in jail, and he is on trial for murder. But he wanted to be a good person. What happened? Who is the real Steve Harmon? What is the truth? Is Steve innocent or is he a monster? There is a vivid contrast between the way Steve would identify himself and the circumstances of the violent situation that led to his imprisonment.

The reality of Steve's situation is based on Myers' research. He spent many hours conducting a series of interviews with prison inmates. When he entered the prison, heard the slam of the heavy steel doors behind him, saw the faces of the young inmates, and experienced the emotions in the visitors' room, he felt he had a sense of the characters, of their situations, and of how they would use language (2001a, 61). It is clear to readers of *Monster* that Myers used the information about the harsh reality of jail life in telling Steve's story. The prison inmates he interviewed, like Steve Harmon, would talk about themselves in the first person. But they would switch to the third person when speaking about the crime, separating themselves from what had happened. Is this separation of self from the crime a way to avoid the truth? "Maybe we are here because we lie to ourselves" (1999b, 203). These words from one of Steve's journal entries show he is considering the possibility. His father, when visiting him in jail, cries and says he never thought he'd see Steve in a place like that. The lady prosecutor calls him a monster; yet his mother says she knows he didn't do anything wrong. But he lies on his cot pondering whether he is fooling himself (148). When the defense attorney turns away after looking at him, he wonders, "what did she see" (281), a decent person or a monster? Who is the real Steve Harmon?

The emotions Myers sensed during his visits to prisons are

conveyed in "Visit" (2003e), a short story that works well with *Monster*. When the father of this unnamed prisoner visits him in jail, the young man, like Steve, talks about his identity, telling his father who he is and is not: "That's not me, man. . . . Hurting people like that" (81). "I don't think I'm all that bad a person" (92). In this story, published in Michael Cart's *Necessary Noise: Stories About Our Families as They Really Are*, the long-absent father is having one last talk, which is like "a babble of confessions" (92), with his son who is on death row.

"Who Am I? Where Is My Place?" Identity and Choices

What one true image shows these young men who they really are? What has led them to be a part of a situation in which someone is murdered during a robbery attempt? Are there ways young people who grow up in an inner-city environment can construct an identity, defining themselves in a way that helps them resist the challenges to their masculinity, the pressures from peers to be tough enough to participate in the action that ends in violence? In the midst of the turmoil of adolescence, what are the consequences of the choices they make? Along with exploring the relationships between father and sons, which is a part of both *Monster* and "Visit," these questions are examples of themes that run through many of Myers' literary works.

Walter Dean Myers is concerned about the violence in schools and communities. From his interviews in prisons, he noted a common thread among many of the inmates: as young people, they had been bullied or abused, which causes them to be isolated and to take on a view of life in which they think hitting people is okay. Because identity develops through one's relationships with others, he explores what connections young people have (Myers 2005b) and whether there is even one person, a parent or a parent figure, who might make a difference in helping them see alternative ways of viewing life and its possibilities and their place in the world.

In many of Myers' stories at least one significant adult tries to help the young person make wise decisions (Bishop 1997, 392).

The assistant coaches in *Hoops* and *Slam!* and the barber in *Handbook for Boys: A Novel* are examples of characters who take on the role of being a model and are the caring adults who give the protagonists advice about the consequences of choices. These adults often see that the young person has the potential to succeed if he or she can resist the pressures from others. When he is in prison, Steve thinks about Mr. Sawicki, his teacher in film class, and what he had learned from this important teacher. Steve is also aware of the love of his parents. Yet he did want to fit in with the young men in his inner-city neighborhood. Disturbing questions about peer pressures, identity, choices, and violence are complex, and the importance of teens having the opportunity to talk about the issues as raised in quality literature cannot be underestimated. It is important to note, however, that violence does not occur only in urban environments. The consequences of young people being bullied and feeling isolated are tragic wherever they occur.

Shooter: What Leads to the Violence?

In the novel *Shooter*, as in *Monster* and "Visit," a crime has taken place before the events depicted in the narrative. *Shooter* is the story of the aftermath of a shooting incident that left two dead and nine wounded, an event with many similarities to the tragedies that occurred in Columbine High School. The book begins with the cold facts in Harrison County School Safety Committee's Threat Analysis Report and ends with the medical examiner's findings. The high school students in *Shooter* are driven by emotional factors they don't really understand. Myers takes a close look at aspects of violence and tries to understand young people and the compelling dynamics that drive them to such desperate acts.

Specifically in *Shooter,* he explores the complexities of the individuals' self-concept, family relationships, the effects of bullying, and how the young people reach out for help. Pieces of the story in *Shooter* are conveyed in Cameron's and Carla's varied answers when they talk with a county psychologist, with a special FBI agent who is a threat assessment analyst, and with a sheriff. Readers also learn much from Len's diary. This "Diary or Journal Found in the Home of Leonard Gray" (167), with its clever wordplay, puns, and mythological references, is part of the last seventy-four pages of the book, which are compiled as appendices. Also included are the police report and various newspaper articles. One article is about the "two young men who never could get together socially [who] were buried on the same day" (155). As in *Monster*, the varied formats and the specific fonts used in *Shooter* match the nature of the words and add to the impact of the story.

Street Love: Taking Responsibility for One's Life

Street Love is another brilliant example of Myers' exploration of the possibilities of language and form and his examination of ways young people take responsibility for their own lives. Again, the protagonists have questions about who they are and how to find their place in the world. *Street Love* is a love story told in free verse, a format that was inspired by Shakespearian iambic pentameter and then loosened up with the cadences and rhythms of rap. Myers' use of unique voices for the various characters in the story is particularly effective (www.walterdeanmyersbooks.com 2006). Set in Harlem, it is a story of urban love between seventeen-year-old Damien, who has been admitted to Brown University, and sixteen-year-old Junice, whose mother is sentenced to twenty-five years in prison for possession and distribution of drugs. Vivid images in the narrative convey much about the setting and the young people growing up in the inner city, such as the "tall Brother working on his gangster lean" (8). In the "hood" there are the bad and the good; some guys like rivals Sledge and Chico know "they can't reach and all they got is hate to lift them from the misery of the day" (7). But Damien is "comfortable in stride and gesture" (2) especially when he is "ball-dancing."

Damien and his friend Kevin are young, proud, and Black, but

Damien doesn't hear any clear message of what tomorrow will bring. Then he meets beautiful, strong, streetwise, and determined Junice. He notes, "She walks darkly, as if her mind weighs down Her steps" (11). Junice's path is very different from the one Damien is expected to follow. They are both aware that their experiences and perspectives are worlds apart. Facing what seems like a hopeless situation, Junice realizes the system will probably not let her and her younger sister Melissa stay with their grandmother who seems unaware of what is really happening. Junice also knows it is going to be hard not to end up like her incarcerated mother. "I am street! My mind and soul are street" (89), she says to herself, but her heart calls out to Damien, who is torn between the dreams his parents have for him and his desire to help her (www.harper collinschildrens.com 2006). Is he the hope that will help her be more than is written in her future? What will Damien do when Junice decides to take her sister and leave for Memphis to live with a distant relative?

Street Love is a beautifully written, lyrical, and touching story. It is also an example of Myers' desire to write books that bridge the reality of urban life and the ideal. He is concerned about how innocent children are betrayed and how they suffer when parents are incarcerated. But he is also impressed with how courageous some young people are, particularly those who are determined to try to break the cycle of failure and not accept being a victim. For Myers, *Street Love* is a "way of recognizing that the human spirit is no less noble because it lives in the inner city" (www.walterdeanmyers books.com 2006), and there are reasons to have hope for the future of these young people.

Classroom Activities

As with all of his books, there are a variety of ways to deepen students' responses to and interpretations of *Monster, Shooter,* and *Street Love*, strategies that in turn also enhance small group and whole class discussion. For example, two approaches that work especially well with middle school readers as well as college students are "Save the Last Word for Me" and a version of "Think, Pair, Share," a strategy that involves exploring issues and/or themes in the story and supporting the ideas with textual evidence. When participating in "Save the Last Word for Me" (Short, Harste, and Burke 1996, 506–11), readers have an opportunity to construct their own interpretations of a story before discussing it with others. In this activity, which works very well for small group discussion, students come to class with a given number of index cards or slips of scrap paper on which they have written quotations from the story that particularly caught their attention. On the back of the cards they write what to them is the significance of the quotation as it relates to the whole story. They arrange the cards in the order of the ones they would most like to discuss. After they read a chosen quotation and peers have an opportunity to react to the quote, the original student has the last word about his or her reason for picking the quotation. Peers often cite why they chose the same passage or something related to it. It is not unusual during the discussion for students to comment that their own understanding of the book is expanded as they hear ideas from others.

"Think, Pair, Share" is an in-class activity that can occur at any point during the reading of a story or after readers have completed reading a work. Because Myers raises many social, legal, and moral issues in *Monster*, such as unresolved perjury and questions about what is the truth, this strategy works very well with the novel. When focusing on issues or themes, one student *thinks* about issues that are a part of the story and writes down a list of them. This list is passed to a peer who must write down specifically what in the story is the textual evidence that supports the original idea. For example with *Monster*, students note issues about inner-city crime, prison life, judicial equality, racial profiling, teens and peer pressure, honesty, and humanization. The two students can either discuss with each other what is on their lists and the specific support from the text or each write a response to the peer's ideas. After the *pair* work, the list is passed back to the original student, who will then choose to *share* either the ideas from his or her original list or what was noted on a peer's list of issues and themes. The whole class discussion is enriched when individual students first think about the issues and themes, expand their ideas with what a peer has said or written, determine what in the text supports the ideas, and then hear what others have thought and shared.

When students participate in one of these classroom activities focused on their reactions to *Monster*, they probe ideas about identity, about Myers' concern about Harlem youth, and about issues of judicial equality. Many readers choose passages in which it is clear Steve had wanted to be macho. For example, in his screenplay he writes about the pressure of having been accused by Osvaldo of being lame (82). In a powerful journal entry, Steve writes, "It was me, I thought as I tried not to throw up, that had wanted to be tough like them" (130). Yet he is a young kid who is scared to death, who feels as though he doesn't have a role in what is happening in the courtroom. Readers note that many adolescents feel like a string puppet, completely out of the process of determining what is happening to them.

Readers note Myers' comments about how the judicial system works. Kathy O'Brien, Steve's lawyer, tells him half the jurors believe he is guilty the moment they see him: "You're young, you're Black, and you're on trial. What else do you need to know?" (79) she says. Steve realizes it is O'Brien's job to try to make him different from Bobo, Osvaldo, and King, the others who were involved in the crime. He is like any teenager trying to find his identity and fit in. He wonders what O'Brien sees when she looks at him. Does he become a monster when he lies in court? He feels the word *Monster* is tattooed on his forehead (61), which is an idea mature readers relate to books such as *The Scarlet Letter* and *A Lesson Before Dying*. With its unique structure and first-person voice, Myers' *Monster* is also an excellent choice to use as a connection to Mary Shelley's *Frankenstein* as readers explore the concept of a monster (Phillips 2003, 87–90). Clearly this multilayered, multitextual, gripping story is rich with possibilities.

The Importance of Literacy

Walter Dean Myers understands the lure of drugs, gangs, and violence when young people have no sense of possibilities available to them, have no hope for a life that is different from what surrounds them, and see no way to attain their dreams. But Myers feels that reading books and writing stories and poems are what saved him. He places a very high value on the gift of stories and of reading. When he interviewed prisoners in various penal institutions, he sought to understand why these people had "gone bad" (Bishop 1991, 17). He noted that many inmates did not have what he had: the gift of literacy. They had rich verbal skills, but not reading skills. He "wants to write for people who are not self-reliant, people who can't get up every day and do the right thing. I want to write for the non-reader" (Ruggieri 2006, 8). But his stories are for all readers.

Myers' frequent appearances with the National Basketball Association's "Read to Achieve" program is one of the ways he shows his concern that all young people develop the love of reading. He also has helped to establish the Walter Dean Myers Publishing Institute, part of the Langston Hughes Children's Literature Festival.

Walter Dean Myers' artistry, his compassion, and his gift with language touch readers of all ages, readers who quickly become immersed in the lives of his characters. For multitudes of readers, Steve Harmon, Fast Sam, Lonnie Jackson, Jamal Hicks, and Richie Perry are as real as Malcolm X, Dr. Martin Luther King, and Muhammad Ali. As Walter Dean Myers continues to expand his craft, he is clearly among those whom he describes when referring to other authors: the "best writers, the ones we return to again and again, [who] invest their stories with layers of meaning so that the reader will come away possessing far more than they did when they first started the book" (Myers 2001a, 62). He is first and foremost a gifted teller of stories. Readers who have discovered the joy of being immersed in one of his stories, whatever the genre, look forward to the many creative projects that will become another wonderful book by Walter Dean Myers. His gift to all people is a deeper understanding of their own story and of the experiences and emotions of all humanity.

WORKS CITED

www.authors4teens.com. 2003. Greenwood Publishing Group, Inc.

www.harpercollinschildrens.com. 2006.

www.walterdeanmyersbooks.com. 2006.

Angelou, Maya. 1993. *Life Doesn't Frighten Me*, illustrated by Jean-Michel Basquiet, edited by Sara Jane Boyers. New York: Stewart, Tabori & Chang.

———. 1994. "Grey Day." In *The Complete Collected Poems of Maya Angelou*, 69. New York: Random House.

Aronson, Marc, Paul Fleischman, Jim Murphy, Harry Mazer, and Walter Dean Myers. 2006. "The Author's Responsibility: Telling the Truth About War." *The ALAN Review* 33 (3): 36–44.

Bishop, Rudine Sims. 1991. *Presenting Walter Dean Myers*. Boston: Twayne Publishers.

———. 1997. "Walter Dean Myers." *Writers for Young Adults*, Vol. 2, edited by Ted Hipple, 387–96. New York: Charles Scribner's Sons.

Book Fair Magic, 1995–1996. 1995. Produced by Scholastic, Inc. 23 minutes, 11 seconds.

Cohan, George M. 1917. "Over There." www.english.emory.edu /LostPoets/OverThere.html.

Crane, Stephen. 1898. "A Mystery of Heroism." 2005. In *Elements of Literature: Fifth Course, Essentials of American Literature*, 435–41. Austin, TX: Holt, Rinehart and Winston.

———. 1899. "War Is Kind." 2005. In *Elements of Literature: Fifth Course, Essentials of American Literature*, 443. Austin, TX: Holt, Rinehart and Winston.

Ehrhart, W. D. 1998a. "Coming Home." In *From Both Sides Now: The Poetry of the Vietnam War and Its Aftermath,* edited by Phillip Mahony, 206. New York: Charles Scribner's Sons.

———. 1998b. "Guerrilla War." In *From Both Sides Now: The Poetry of the Vietnam War and Its Aftermath,* edited by Phillip Mahony, 61. New York: Charles Scribner's Sons.

———. 1998c. "The Next Step." In *From Both Sides Now: The Poetry of the Vietnam War and Its Aftermath,* edited by Phillip Mahony, 57. New York: Charles Scribner's Sons.

Evan, Thomas, Tamara Lipper, Michael Isikoff, Daniel Klaidman, Susannah Meadows, and Jill Jordan Sieder. 2004. "A Quagmire . . . in the Making? The Vietnam Question." *Newsweek* 143 (16): 24–35.

Forrest Gump. 1995. Produced by Steve Tisch, Wendy Finerman, and Steve Starkey. Directed by Robert Zemeckis. 142 minutes. Paramount Pictures. Videocassette.

Gallo, Donald R., ed. 1990. *Speaking for Ourselves: Autobiographical Sketches by Notable Authors of Books for Young Adults.* Urbana, IL: NCTE.

Giovanni, Nikki. 1985. "The Drum." In *Spin a Soft Black Song: Poems for Children,* illustrated by George Martins. New York: Hill and Wang.

Glenn, Mel. 1988. *Back to Class.* New York: Clarion.

Hemingway, Ernest. 1925. "Soldier's Home." From *In Our Time.* New York: Charles Scribner's Sons. 2005. In *Elements of Literature: Fifth Course, Essentials of American Literature,* 611–17. Austin, TX: Holt, Rinehart and Winston.

Hughes, Langston. 1995. *The Block: Poems.* New York: Viking.

Jennings, Peter. 1999. *The Century: America's Time.* Produced by ABC News and The History Channel.

Johannessen, Larry R. 1992. *Illumination Rounds: Teaching the Literature of the Vietnam War.* Urbana, IL: NCTE.

———. 1993. "Young-Adult Literature and the Vietnam War." *English Journal* 82 (5): 43–49.

———. 2002. "When History Talks Back: Teaching Nonfiction Literature of the Vietnam War." *English Journal* 91 (4): 39–47.

Kazemek, Francis E. 1998. "The Things They Carried: Vietnam War Literature by and About Women in the Secondary Classroom." *Journal of Adolescent and Adult Literacy* 42 (3): 156–65.

Kessinger, Mark. 1998. "Dead." In *From Both Sides Now: The Poetry of the Vietnam War and Its Aftermath,* edited by Phillip Mahony, 118. New York: Charles Scribner's Sons.

Mahony, Phillip, ed. 1998. *From Both Sides Now: The Poetry of the Vietnam War and Its Aftermath.* New York: Charles Scribner's Sons.

Meek, Nancy. 2001. "A Grateful Heart." http://namtour.com /response.html.

Myers, Walter Dean. 1969. *Where Does the Day Go?,* illustrated by Leo Carty. New York: Parents Magazine Press.

———. 1972. *The Dragon Takes a Wife,* illustrated by Ann Grifalconi. Indianapolis: Bobbs-Merrill.

———. 1975. *Fast Sam, Cool Clyde, and Stuff.* New York: Puffin.

———. 1977. *Mojo and the Russians.* New York: Viking.

———. 1978. *It Ain't All for Nothin'.* New York: Viking.

———. 1979. *The Young Landlords.* New York: Viking.

———. 1981. *Hoops.* New York: Dell.

———. 1982. *Won't Know Till I Get There.* New York: Viking.

———. 1983. "The Treasure of Lemon Brown." In *Boy's Life* (March); 1993, *Read* 43 (5): 4–9.

———. 1984a. *Motown and Didi: A Love Story.* New York: Viking.

———. 1984b. *The Outside Shot.* New York: Delacorte.

———. 1987a. *Crystal.* New York: Amistad/HarperCollins.

———. 1987b. "Jeremiah's Song." In *Visions: Nineteen Short Stories by Outstanding Writers for Young Adults,* edited by Donald R. Gallo, 194–202. New York: Delacorte.

———. 1988a. *Fallen Angels.* New York: Scholastic.

———. 1988b. *Scorpions.* New York: Harper & Row.

———. 1988c. "The Young Adult Novel: Writing for Aliens." Speech presented at the breakfast meeting of the Assembly on Literature for Adolescents, Seventy-Eighth Annual Convention of the National Council of Teachers of English, November 19, St. Louis, Missouri.

———. 1990a. *Cages.* In *Center Stage: One-Act Plays for Teenage Readers and Actors,* edited by Donald R. Gallo, 300–30. New York: HarperCollins.

———. 1990b. *The Mouse Rap.* New York: HarperCollins.

———. 1991a. "Cultural Substance: A Writer's Gift to Readers." In *The Multicolored Mirror: Cultural Substance in Literature for Children and*

Young Adults, edited by Merri V. Lindgren, 117–23. Fort Atkinson, WI: Highsmith Press.

———. 1991b. *Now Is Your Time! The African American Struggle for Freedom*. New York: HarperCollins.

———. 1992a. *The Righteous Revenge of Artemis Bonner*. New York: HarperCollins.

———. 1992b. *Somewhere in the Darkness*. New York: Scholastic.

———. 1992c. Speech at the Assembly on Literature for Adolescents Workshop, November 18, Louisville, Kentucky.

———. 1993a. *Brown Angels: An Album of Pictures and Verse*. New York: HarperCollins.

———. 1993b. *Malcolm X: By Any Means Necessary*. New York: Scholastic.

———. 1994. *The Glory Field*. New York: Scholastic.

———. 1995a. *Glorious Angels: A Celebration of Children*. New York: HarperCollins.

———. 1995b. *One More River to Cross: An African American Photograph Album*. New York: Harcourt Brace & Company.

———. 1996a. "Reverend Abbott and Those Bloodshot Eyes." In *When I Was Your Age: Original Stories About Growing Up*, edited by Amy Ehrlich, 65–76. Cambridge, MA: Candlewick.

———. 1996b. *Slam!* New York: Scholastic.

———. 1997a. "Briefcase." In *Twelve Shots: Outstanding Short Stories About Guns*, edited by Harry Mazer, 7–23. New York: Delacorte.

———. 1997b. *Harlem: A Poem*, illustrated by Christopher Myers. New York: Scholastic.

———. 1997c. "Stranger." In *No Easy Answers: Short Stories About Teenagers Making Tough Choices*, edited by Donald R. Gallo, 209–24. New York: Delacorte.

———. 1998a. *Amistad: A Long Road to Freedom*. New York: Dutton.

———. 1998b. *Angel to Angel: A Mother's Gift of Love*. New York: HarperCollins.

———. 1999a. *At Her Majesty's Request: An African Princess in Victorian England*. New York: Scholastic.

———. 1999b. *Monster*. New York: HarperCollins.

———. 2000a. *The Blues of Flats Brown*, illustrated by Nina Laden. New York: Holiday House.

———. 2000b. *Malcolm X: A Fire Burning Brightly*, illustrated by Leonard Jenkins. New York: HarperCollins.

———. 2000c. *145th Street: Short Stories*. New York: Delacorte.

———. 2001a. "And Then I Read. . . ." *Voices from the Middle* 8 (4): 58–62.

———. 2001b. *Bad Boy: A Memoir*. New York: HarperCollins.

———. 2001c. *The Greatest: Muhammad Ali*. New York: Scholastic.

———. 2002a. *Handbook for Boys: A Novel*. New York: HarperCollins.

———. 2002b. *Patrol: An American Soldier in Vietnam*, illustrated by Ann Grifalconi. New York: HarperCollins.

———. 2003a. *The Beast*. New York: Scholastic.

———. 2003b. *Blues Journey*, illustrated by Christopher Myers. New York: Holiday House.

———. 2003c. *The Dream Bearer*. New York: HarperCollins.

———. 2003d. *A Time to Love: Stories from the Old Testament*, illustrated by Christopher Myers. New York: Scholastic.

———. 2003e. "Visit." In *Necessary Noise: Stories About Our Families as They Really Are*, edited by Michael Cart, 83–95. New York: HarperCollins.

———. 2004a. *Antarctica: Journeys to the South Pole*. New York: Scholastic.

———. 2004b. *Here in Harlem: Poems in Many Voices*. New York: Holiday House.

———. 2004c. *I've Seen the Promised Land: The Life of Dr. Martin Luther King, Jr.*, illustrated by Leonard Jenkins. New York: HarperCollins.

———. 2004d. *Shooter*. New York: Amistad/HarperCollins.

———. 2004e. *USS Constellation: Pride of the American Navy*. New York: Holiday House.

———. 2005a. *Autobiography of My Dead Brother*. New York: Tempest/Amistad.

———. 2005b. Meet the Author. Session at the Ohio Council Teachers of English Arts Spring Conference, March 4, Columbus, Ohio.

———. 2005c. Panel Presentation at the Assembly on Literature for Adolescents Workshop, November 21, Pittsburgh, Pennsylvania.

———. 2005d. "Writing for the Uninspired Reader." *English Journal* 94 (3): 36–38.

———. 2006a. *Jazz*, illustrated by Christopher Myers. New York: Holiday House.

———. 2006b. *Street Love*. New York: Amistad.

Myers, Walter Dean, and Bill Miles. 2006. *The Harlem Hellfighters: When Pride Met Courage*. New York: HarperCollins.

Phillips, Nathan. 2003. "*Monsters'* Ink: How Walter Dean Myers Made *Frankenstein* Fun (Young Adult Literature)." *English Journal* 92 (6): 87–90.

Rinaldi, Denise. 1993. "Walter Dean Myers Finds His Roots." *Scholastic Scope* (March 26).

Ruggieri, Colleen. 2006. "Life, Learning and Young Adult Literature: A Conversation with Walter Dean Myers." *Ohio Journal of English Language Arts* 46 (2): 7–11.

Short, Kathy G., Jerome C. Harste, and Carolyn Burke. 1996. *Creating Classrooms for Authors and Inquirers*. 2nd ed. 506–11. Portsmouth, NH: Heinemann.

We Were Soldiers. 2002. Produced by Bruce Davey, Stephen McEveety and Randall Wallace. Directed by Randall Wallace. 138 minutes. Paramount Pictures and Icon Productions. Videocassette.

Walter Dean Myers Books Cited: Listed by Genre

Novels

Fast Sam, Cool Clyde, and Stuff (1975)

Mojo and the Russians (1977)

It Ain't All for Nothin' (1978)

The Young Landlords (1979)

Hoops (1981)

Won't Know Till I Get There (1982)

Motown and Didi: A Love Story (1984)

The Outside Shot (1984)

Crystal (1987)

Fallen Angels (1988)

Scorpions (1988)

The Mouse Rap (1990)

The Righteous Revenge of Artemis Bonner (1992)

Somewhere in the Darkness (1992)
The Glory Field (1994)
Slam! (1996)
Monster (1999)
Handbook for Boys: A Novel (2002)
The Beast (2003)
The Dream Bearer (2003)
Shooter (2004)
Autobiography of My Dead Brother (2005)
Street Love (2006)

Nonfiction

Now Is Your Time! The African American Struggle for Freedom (1991)
Malcolm X: By Any Means Necessary (1993)
One More River to Cross: An African American Photograph Album (1995)
Harlem: A Poem (1997)
Amistad: A Long Road to Freedom (1998)
At Her Majesty's Request: An African Princess in Victorian England (1999)
Bad Boy: A Memoir (2001)
The Greatest: Muhammad Ali (2001)
Antarctica: Journeys to the South Pole (2004)
USS Constellation: Pride of the American Navy (2004)
The Harlem Hellfighters: When Pride Met Courage (2006)

Picture Books

Where Does the Day Go? (1969)
The Dragon Takes a Wife (1972)
The Blues of Flats Brown (2000)
Malcolm X: A Fire Burning Brightly (2000)
Blues Journey (2003)
A Time to Love: Stories from the Old Testament (2003)
I've Seen the Promised Land: The Life of Dr. Martin Luther King, Jr. (2004)
Jazz (2006)

Poetry

Brown Angels: An Album of Pictures and Verse (1993)

Glorious Angels: A Celebration of Children (1995)
Angel to Angel: A Mother's Gift of Love (1998)
Patrol: An American Soldier in Vietnam (2002)
Here in Harlem: Poems in Many Voices (2004)

Short Stories
"The Treasure of Lemon Brown" (1983)
"Jeremiah's Song" (1987)
"Reverend Abbott and Those Bloodshot Eyes" (1996)
"Briefcase" (1997)
"Stranger" (1997)
145th Street: Short Stories (2000)
"Visit" (2003)

Play
Cages (1990)